Life Begins with Faith

Poems and Meditations

by

George W. Wiseman, B.R.E., S.T.M.

First Fruits Press
Wilmore, Kentucky
c2012

ISBN: 9781621710301

Life Begins with Faith: Poems and Meditations, George W. Wiseman
First Fruits Press, © 2012
Previously published by the Author, c1941.

Digital version at http://place.asburyseminary.edu/firstfruitsbooks/5/

First Fruits Press is a digital imprint of the Asbury Theological Seminary, B.L. Fisher Library. Asbury Theological Seminary is the legal owner of the material previously published by the Pentecostal Publishing Co. and reserves the right to release new editions of this material as well as new material produced by Asbury Theological Seminary. Its publications are available for noncommercial and educational uses, such as research, teaching and private study. First Fruits Press has licensed the digital version of this work under the Creative Commons Attribution Noncommercial 3.0 United States License. To view a copy of this license, visit http://creativecommons.org/licenses/by-nc/3.0/us/.

For all other uses, contact:

First Fruits Press
B.L. Fisher Library
Asbury Theological Seminary
204 N. Lexington Ave.
Wilmore, KY 40390
http://place.asburyseminary.edu/firstfruits

Wiseman, George W.
    Life begins with faith : poems and meditations / George W. Wiseman.
    Wilmore, Ky. : First Fruits Press, c2012.
    195 p. : port. ; 21 cm.
    Reprint. Previously published: [Oak Bluffs, Mass. : The Author], c1941
    ISBN: 9781621710301 (pbk.)
    1. Meditations. 2. Christian poetry. I. Title.
BV4832 .W57 2012

Cover design by David Roux

asburyseminary.edu
800.2ASBURY
204 North Lexington Avenue
Wilmore, Kentucky 40390

LIFE BEGINS WITH FAITH

Poems and Meditations

Copyright, 1941, by
GEORGE W. WISEMAN, B.R.E., S T.M.

Printed in the United States of America

LIFE BEGINS WITH FAITH

POEMS and MEDITATIONS

GEORGE W WISEMAN, B. R. E., S. T. M.

FOREWORD

The poems in this volume have been written over a period of years. A greater part of them have been published in various books, magazines and anthologies of verse.

The Meditations are an afterthought, the product of the zero hour. Then in the midst of preparation came a serious illness in the family which silenced my typewriter for months. After a brief respite, Mrs. Wiseman again underwent three major operations in rapid succession. At this moment she hovers between life and death, but her ardent desire is that this book, delayed so long, be published. I trust there will not be revealed, to too great an extent, the haste in which each meditation was written, and the mental anguish that was ever present.

I deeply appreciate everything done by the doctors and hospital of Martha's Vineyard, the surgeons of the Lahey Clinic of Boston, and the New England Deaconess Hospital. We shall never forget the prayers and words of encouragement from the many friends of our various churches, especially those of the Vineyard, whose only demand has been that I remain by the side of my wife.

My prayer as I send forth this volume is that the minister might find some help for the church year, the sorrowful find comfort, faith reborn, and love and devotion to the Master be increased through the reading of these pages.

GEORGE W. WISEMAN

Methodist Parsonage
Oak Bluffs, Mass.
August, 1941

To my wife,
ELSIE MARGARET WISEMAN,
an illustration of an inspiring meditation,
and JOANNE BERYL,
the most perfect example of an unfolding poem,
this volume is lovingly dedicated.

TABLE OF CONTENTS

THE COMING YEAR	14
WHICH WAY ARE WE HEADED?	15
WHAT MAKES A NEW YEAR NEW?	16
WHAT DOES?	17
THE SAVIOUR GOETH BEFORE YOU	18
HE LEADETH ME	19
ABRAHAM LINCOLN	20
WANTED — MODERN LINCOLNS!	21
JOHN WESLEY	22
MEN WHO LIVE	23
DRIFTING	24
ARE WE TOO EASY WITH OURSELVES?	25
ARE WE CERTAIN?	26
DO WE MEAN IT?	27
TOMORROW	28
TOMORROWS THAT NEVER COME	29
THE CHURCH I LIKE	30
THIS IS THE CHURCH	31
WHAT OUR CHURCH SHOULD BE	32
DOES YOUR CHURCH MIND ITS BUSINESS?	33
MY CHURCH	34
IF HE SHOULD COME!	35
TO SEE THE END	36
HOW BIG IS OUR FAITH?	37
AT THE CROSS	38
HOW DO WE LOOK AT THE CROSS?	39
HIS CROSS — MY CROSS	40
OUR CROSS	41
THE REPENTANCE OF PETER	42
HE DID IT!	43
BECAUSE CHRIST DIED	44
HIS GIFT TO ME	45
THE REMORSE OF JUDAS	46
THE MAN WHO COULDN'T TAKE IT	47
THE END THAT NEVER CAME	48
WHAT PETER DID NOT SEE	49
THE FIRST EASTER	50

TABLE OF CONTENTS — Continued

CHRIST LIVES! DO YOU?	51
EASTER THOUGHTS	52
EASTER ALOOFNESS	53
EASTER QUESTIONS	54
MORE EASTER QUESTIONS	55
SINCE CHRIST AROSE	56
WHAT WAS BORN AT EASTER?	57
THE WORLD NEEDS MEN	58
GOD, GIVE US MEN!	59
GIVE ME A FRIEND	60
MAKE WAY FOR YOUR FRIENDS	61
A MOTHER'S LOVE	62
HIS MOTHER'S GOD	63
MOTHER	64
DO NOT FAIL HER	65
MEMORIAL DAY	66
THE FORWARD LOOK OF MEMORIAL DAY	67
I WONDER	68
I BELIEVE IN AMERICA FIRST	69
WHEN THEY HAD PRAYED	70
WHAT DO YOU EXPECT?	71
MY PRAYER	72
I BELIEVE IN PRAYER	73
A PASTOR'S PRAYER	74
FAITH MARCHES ON!	75
WHEN TO PRAY	76
A PRAYING DOCTOR	77
WHO WANTS THE KINGDOM?	78
WELL, WHO DOES?	79
MY SIN	80
THE SIN OF THE MULTITUDE	81
OUR MASTER	82
A COLORED CHRIST	83
IN CHRIST	84
THE WORLD'S MOST TROUBLESOME RELIGION	85
OUR MONEY	86
WHAT IS WORTH WHILE?	87

TABLE OF CONTENTS — Continued

TOGETHER	88
WHOM GOD HATH JOINED TOGETHER	89
TOGETHER STILL	90
WHEN SEPARATION IS IMPOSSIBLE	91
MISUNDERSTOOD	92
WHAT HURTS MOST?	93
POEMS	94
POEMS OF POWER	95
GOD'S ANSWER	96
GOD DOES SPEAK!	97
THE PRICE OF WAR	98
MAN'S INHUMANITY TO MAN	99
ARMISTICE DAY	100
WE ARE STILL SLAVES	101
TWO GODS	102
THE GODS SPEAK	103
THE VOICE OF EUROPE	104
IT MUSTN'T HAPPEN HERE!	105
IF MEN MUST KILL	106
ONWARD, CHRISTIAN SOLDIERS	107
THE FRUIT OF PEACE	108
MAN'S BID FOR PEACE	109
THE BIBLE	110
THE BIBLE FINDS US	111
THE END OF THE DAY	112
THE END THAT DOES COME	113
IF WE BUT KNEW	114
THE PRODIGAL'S BROTHER	115
THE THINGS WE LEAVE UNDONE	116
TAKING OUR OWN MEASURE	117
IF WE BUT HAD A DAY	118
THE BIG TWO LETTER WORD	119
TOO LATE	120
THERE'S SOMETHING WRONG!	121
FORSAKEN	122
WHAT'S THE USE!	123
DO NOT GIVE UP	124

TABLE OF CONTENTS — Continued

WHAT'S THE DIFFERENCE!	125
SHADOWS	126
LIFE'S SHADOW HOURS	127
THE WAY OF THE FATHER	128
WHAT DOES GOD CARE?	129
WE'LL UNDERSTAND	130
CHRISTIAN'S ARE DIFFERENT!	131
NOT DEATH, BUT LIFE	132
THE LIFE THAT LIVES	133
DEATH AS A FRIEND	134
LIFE IN DISGUISE	135
THE HEART OF DEATH	136
THE HEART THAT NEVER STOPS	137
DEATH GIVES	138
WHAT IS THERE LEFT TO DISCOVER?	139
THY WILL BE DONE	140
FAITH FOR DESPERATE DAYS	141
SLEEP ON, BELOVED ONE	142
AS HEAVEN VIEWS IT	143
HEAVEN	144
GOING HOME	145
BE CALM, MY SOUL	146
WATCH YOUR PULSE!	147
OUR THANKS	148
EYES THAT SEE	149
THANKSGIVING THOUGHTS	150
GOD SAVE AMERICA!	151
A THANKSGIVING PRAYER	152
LET US GIVE THANKS	153
OUR DREAMS	154
DREAMERS, PLUS	155
THE CONCEITED MAN	156
THE WORLD'S PICTURE OF YOU	157
HAVE YOU COUNTED THE COST?	158
WHAT IS THE COST?	159
"I HEARD" AND "THEY SAY"	160
THE WORLD'S GREATEST ASSASSINS	161

TABLE OF CONTENTS — Continued

A Selfish Man's Dream	162
The Curse Of The Ages	163
The Rich Young Man	164
Just A Youth	165
Two Men	166
Watch Your Companions!	167
The Widow's Mite	168
What Makes One Rich?	169
The Youth I Like	170
What Price Youth!	171
If I Were Twenty-One	172
Youth To Match The Age	173
Youth's Prayer	174
Youth Can Pray!	175
If Christmas Comes	176
Will We Be Ready?	177
A Shepherd Speaks	178
In Which Direction Are We Looking?	179
No Room	180
Have We Received Jesus?	181
Why Did God Send His Son?	182
We Know The Answer, But — !	183
Because Christ Came	184
What Have We Given?	185
Then And Now	186
Babe Or Saviour, Which?	187
The Leadership Of Love	188
Reserve Resistance	189
A Voice For God	190
Let God Speak	191
The Meaning Of Yesterday	192
Thank God For Yesterday!	193
The Passing Year	194
What Should Die With The Dying Year?	195

Many of the poems in this volume have been revised. In some cases verses have been omitted. This will explain the reason why they appear in a different form than when previously published.

THE COMING YEAR

Another year to stand and watch
  The old year passing in review;
And then to know before us lies
  Another chance to start anew.

Another year for us to mold
  Our lives according to His will;
Another year in which to find
  The place that we alone can fill.

Another year prepares for all
  A book with pages clean and white,
And what we do or leave undone
  Determines what its hand will write.

Another year, and may it be
  A year when poverty will cease
To stalk the world as in the past;
  When war shall be replaced by peace.

Another year has rolled around
  And from its birth moves quickly on;
So let us challenge each new day,
  For time will soon mark this year "gone."

WHICH WAY ARE WE HEADED?

This is Watch Night. At midnight the bells of our church will signify the end of one year and the birth of another. Will it be for the world and the individual a new born year or a still born year? Which way are we headed? The direction can be backwards, in a circle, or forward into the future.

What is it that we see through the gay decorations and above the din of the hour? Do we see a multitude seeking thrills? Gay parties, brawls, noise and general confusion? Our churches will receive a comfortable number of worshippers. Our night clubs will be filled to capacity with hundreds turned away.

Is there anything new in this? Has not every year started thus? If this is all that tonight and tomorrow means, as far as the world and the individual is concerned it will be only another year. A year without the semblance of new life.

But the coming year means more than the few hours that mark its beginning. It has within it twelve new months. What an opportunity for spiritual and mental growth! In the face of this shall we maintain the same spiritual level? Shall we carry into the new year the same prejudices, the same limited vision? Will we be as well satisfied with ourselves as in the past? If so this year will become drab, stilted, allowing only the calendar and the physical side of our life to change. This new year will be but the old year continued.

WHAT MAKES A NEW YEAR NEW?

What make a New Year new?
Not ringing bells or changing dates,
For these soon cease, but not the weights
Of tyranny or lust and greed
On which small men and nations feed;
The world grows big when love controls
Its grasping, hardened, shrunken souls,
This makes a New Year new.

What makes a New Year new?
Not smug contentment with the past,
The mold in which earth's wrongs are cast;
But prophets, unafraid, alive,
To match the age; great souls who strive
To furnish for man's highest good
True justice, peace, and brotherhood.
This makes a New Year new.

What makes a New Year new?
Not resolutions lightly made,
Or worthless dreams born but to fade;
But faith in Christ instead of fate,
More room for God and less for hate;
The world receives its second birth
When God through Christ controls the earth.
This makes a New Year new.

WHAT DOES?

"A happy New Year." How many times have you heard these words today? What will make this year both "happy" and "new" for us? May we consider a few suggestions.

First, there must be a sincere desire to change. There are two ways in which this change can be effected. One way is to start over again. Unfortunately this cannot always be done, especially in the realm where our greatest mistakes and failures are made. The second way is is to accept the conditions of life and change them until they fit into God's plan. Jesus did this. He took the common things of life and so changed them that they became God-like.

Again, if this is to be a "new year," it will come only by making new men and new women. There is no magic in changing the calendar. There is magic in changing the human heart. The secret of a new year rests upon my heart, your heart and every heart in the universe. We must be born again.

To make a New Year new requires not only new individuals but also new churches. The New Year comes to our church like a burst of sunlight, but we have developed only a few souls to challenge it.

Nations are to be born again if this year is to be new. The same old unregenerate nations equals the same greed, distrust, misunderstandings, war. We must be reborn in every area of life if this year is to be new.

THE SAVIOUR GOETH BEFORE YOU

The Saviour goeth before you,
  So what if your path be dim?
Your greatest fear of the future
  Is encountered first by Him;
And thus like the faithful shepherd
  Who goeth before his sheep,
He leads you in perfect safety,
  Though rough be your road and steep.

The Saviour goeth before you,
  Fear not, then, approaching night;
That which is hidden by darkness
  Escapes not the Master's sight.
And when the dread hand of sorrow
  Darkens your limited view,
Remember, it first meets Jesus
  Before it encounters you.

The Saviour goeth before you
  By night as well as by day,
Removing fears of a lifetime
  That marked each step of your way.
Then cease from your needless worry;
  Fear not what life holds in store;
Let this be your consolation,
  Your Saviour goeth before.

HE LEADETH ME

The Saviour not only goes before me preparing a way through the problems, difficulties and dangers of life over which I can safely pass, but even after the road is prepared He is still my leader. He never casts me adrift. He does not want me to lose my way. His hand is always extended in my direction. The responsibility of accepting Him as my leader rests with me.

Sometimes He becomes severe in His leadership. Often, for my own protection, "He maketh me to lie down in green pastures." Only in this way can I achieve poise and inner calm sufficient to overcome the pressure of this turbulent hour.

He is always consistent. "He leadeth me," not occasionally, but constantly. Many times have I sought to lead Him. His way did not seem to be the most attractive for the modern day. Sometimes I have impatiently left Him behind. How slow He seemed to one accustomed to speed. But always when I returned He was still ready to lead. He did not become impatient with me.

He satisfies. "He leadeth me beside the still waters" and "in paths of righteousness." He ushers me in quiet places that I might have the opportunity to think and meditate that the world does not give. Church worship, communion, private devotions, the study of God's Word —these are the waters that refresh me. The paths that are right may not be easy in an age that revels in short-cuts and detours, but only as I follow Him will I in turn be fit to follow.

> *"He leadeth me! O blessed thought!*
> *O words with heavenly comfort fraught!*
> *What-e're I do, wher-e're I be,*
> *Still 'tis God's hand that leadeth me."*

ABRAHAM LINCOLN

God gave him sight.
He looked beneath the surface of man's skin
And saw that outward color did not change
The heart within.

God gave him strength.
He welcomed it, then stooped to lift the weight
That greedy hands had shaped through prejudice
And human hate.

God gave him life.
He took it from God's hands with heart aglow,
Then laid it at the feet of men whose names
He did not know.

He worked with God.
And when his sun set in the western sky,
Its rays illumined earth with freedom's light
That could not die.

WANTED — MODERN LINCOLN'S!

The demand of the hour is for men. Not men who are ever on the march, with weapons of death and destruction held tightly in their hands. They are the slaves of this age, unable to think, act or speak for themselves. The need of the hour is for men, built upon the lines of Abraham Lincoln, who will emancipate mankind from this ancient slavery from which the world has never been freed.

Lincoln was courageous. It was courage born of conviction. He was unafraid of the difficulties of life. He faced and mastered them, from his boyhood in a log cabin, to the fateful moment of his assassination. Our need is for men who will rise courageously above the multiple difficulties of this day.

He loved right and hated wrong. He was opposed to anything that shackled men. Our modern Lincoln must be one who will support everything right and become the enemy of everything wrong.

He abhorred pretense. He cared nothing for pomp and show. The atmosphere surrounding our present day dictators would have been obnoxious to him. Is there any wonder that the world is praying for men, free from the destructive thirst for power and fame, who will once again lead us in paths of righteousness?

He was always sympathetic. His own sorrows made him feel keenly the sorrows of others. He never lost his head. In the face of confusion and hysteria of his day he remained calm. He was sure his ideals would triumph.

Above all he was deeply religious. He possessed what we need. The demand of the hour is for men—like Lincoln.

JOHN WESLEY

With heart warmed by the fires of Aldersgate,
Possessed with courage, zeal, and self-control,
He made religion live, and as he preached
Men felt the power of his flaming soul.

He looked upon a world grown old in sin,
Where God and man walked often far apart;
He made that world his parish, and in time
Had placed the cross of Christ upon its heart.

He pioneered in unaccustomed ways,
His pulpit rose wherever people flocked;
He moved religion from secluded halls
Into the stream of life where mankind walked.

He ended life, the center of his age,
A giant soul within a weakened frame,
Who found burnt embers of a waning faith,
And left a million altar fires aflame.

MEN WHO LIVE

This is a poem but not a meditation on John Wesley. It is an appreciation of the founders of all denominations. As Christians, we cherish their names and rejoice in their fervor and earnestness. They made Christ real to the world and brought consolation to the hearts of multitudes. As Protestants, we accept as our own all who blazed a trail in the wilderness of unrighteousness. They belong, not to one church, but to all churches.

Their consecration and devotion to the Master saved them. No matter how ineffective they were in their early ministry, when once their hearts became strangely warmed, they became examples of effectiveness. They made more enemies than friends, but they were able to mold the lives of their friends to such a degree that they soon possessed their zeal and passion.

They adventured in unaccustomed ways. This is always hard. To conform to accepted standards is natural, but to do that which is different is difficult.

Their unswerving loyalty to the truth saved the nations in which they ministered. Whatever strength is to be found in any Christian nation, came not through the efforts of rulers or armies, but through these flaming evangels who would not rest until the ills of their day were remedied.

They saved religion. Altar fires were rekindled everywhere. A religious impetus was started that was guaranteed to live.

May we pause and pay tribute today to these disciples of the Master who have made it possible for us to worship as we desire.

DRIFTING

I stood one day in early Spring
  Upon a windswept beach,
And saw a tossing, unmanned boat
  Drift clear of human reach.
It seemed the northeast gale rejoiced
  As eagerly it bore
The drifting, bobbing, half-filled boat,
  Further away from shore.
Further away from shore, unmanned,
Drifting wherever the winds command.

I thought as I retraced my steps,
  How like that unmanned boat,
Are they who choose to drift through life,
  Who struggle not — just float.
I thought how sad the ending when
  Their drifting days were o'er,
To learn, too late, how far their course
  Had carried them from shore.
Drifting ever upon life's sea,
Never the men God meant them to be.

The raging sea is life itself,
  No soul escapes its force;
Where men must toil, but never drift
  From off God's chartered course.
The friendly shore is where God dwells,
  Where faith and strength abide,
And they who drift float ever out,
  Far from the Father's side.
Far from the Father's side today,
Means casting Eternal Life away.

ARE WE TOO EASY WITH OURSELVES?

Some years ago, while Pastor of the Methodist Church in Scituate Harbor, Massachusetts, I stood upon the shore and watched the drifting boat that inspired this poem. It was during a severe northeast storm, that in some sections of North Scituate, sent the waves crashing over the sea wall and the roofs of summer cottages near by. As I watched I noticed a small boat that had broken from its mooring. It looked like an apple bobbing in the water. Men were too busy to bother with this craft and so it was allowed to go on its giddy, reckless way. It soon became partly filled with water and on several occasions appeared as though it would sink. However, when I left, it still could be seen drifting crazily about, always widening the distance between it and its mooring.

The thought came to me, "How much like the drifter that I had preached about and referred to many times from my pulpit!" Yes, and I not only preached about that drifter, but I had seen him. I had watched him as he staggered into Morgan Memorial in Boston. I had prayed with him at the altar of the Dover Street Rescue Mission. I had preached to him in jail. And always in private interview I had found this, that at one time that broken piece of driftwood was once a noble vessel. He was securely anchored at some mooring. Then came an exceptionally severe northeast gale. He had weathered many of them. Some not too successfully, but enough to get by, but this one was different. It was a temptation made to order and he trusted in himself instead of in God. He was too easy with himself. He broke away from his mooring to spend a life drifting.

ARE WE CERTAIN?

Are we certain when we whisper
　"Not my will but Thine be done,"
That tomorrow will not witness
　Our will still the strongest one?

Do we mean it when we answer
　"Here am I, O Lord, send me?
When His cause has been forsaken
　Will we also turn and flee?

Are we certain when we promise
　To leave all and follow Him,
That the zeal of consecration
　Will not wane when hope grows dim?

It is not enough to follow
　When the road is bright ahead;
Only those are true who labor
　When the multitude has fled.

DO WE MEAN IT?

Although most of us are sincere when we promise the Master to labor in His vineyard, we sometimes act as though our fingers were crossed when the promise was made.

If we mean it we will soon prove to the world that we were not just talking. We will act as though we care. We will do that which we have long left undone, and will leave undone much that formally occupied our time. The world always knows when we are talking, because it fails to see a noticeable change in our actions.

If we mean it when we pray, "Thy will be done," we will be haunted by the thought that we must do His will. Experience has taught us, that if we expect God to answer our prayers, we must give Him all the help needed. We cannot view this petition in a different light. It will not answer itself. To merely repeat it on Sunday and forget it on Monday, is either a constant reflection on our cold indifference or our woeful weakness.

If we mean it when we say, "Here am I, send me," then we must recognize that God has a right to control our lives. This is not always easy. We resent the control of others. We would rather govern ourselves. Yet have we not placed ourselves at His disposal? Self must be forgotten. God must have all there is of us.

If we mean it we will say with Doctor Earl Marlatt,

> " 'Lord, we are able.' Our spirits are Thine.
> Remold them, make us, like Thee, divine.
> Thy guiding radiance above us shall be
> A beacon to God, to love and loyalty."

TOMORROW

One day the Lord gave me a job to do.
But I had other selfish plans in view,
And so I said, "Lord, I will work for you,
Tomorrow."

The next day dawned. The Lord's job faced me still;
Once more I met Him with my stubborn will,
And answered, "Lord, you'll have to wait until,
Tomorrow."

And still another day passed swiftly by;
I knew the job was there for me to try,
But once again I gave the same reply,
"Tomorrow."

Tomorrow came. The job was never done,
For I had whispered 'ere the day begun,
"I'll do it, Lord, before the setting sun
Tomorrow."

Then suddenly it seemed the Lord had gone;
He wanted one He could depend upon
To do His work today; not shove it on
Tomorrow.

Too late I learned how selfish, mean and rude
I was to Him; yet haughty and unmoved
I offered only as my gratitude,
"Tomorrow."

I know that when I face some crucial day
When I the Lord will need without delay,
He will not glance at me and vaguely say,
"Tomorrow."

So now when'ere the Lord reads off my name
For work He'd have me do, I'll not complain,
Or let my stubborn will and tongue exclaim,
"Tomorrow."

TOMORROWS THAT NEVER COME

Most of the poems in this volume were suggested by some event or experience. This one is different. The suggestion came from another poem, "Too Busy," by Paul Laurence Dunbar. His poem deals with one who considerd himself too busy to do the Lord's work. He promptly informs God to either get someone else or wait until he got through. But the day of emergency arrived. He needed God and in that hour he felt the sting of an accusing conscience. Paul Laurence Dunbar ends his poem with these significant words, "Nobody else can do the work that God's marked out for you."

How easy it is to allow the unimportant to stand in the way of the work that God expects us to do today! That which is pleasant and attractive is often more appealing than that which God requires. We place on the shoulders of tomorrow the work that should be done today.

Tomorrow! What an alluring word! What a convenient rack on which to place that which we do not desire to challenge today! Youth looks at tomorrow and sees unlimited opportunities. He is, to a certain extent, right. But what opportunities are missed by overlooking the present! Too often for him the tomorrow he longs for never comes.

The man of the world sees his "break" in tomorrow. Good luck will come his way. Fortune will smile upon him. How blind he is to the fortune that faces him today! His golden tomorrow might never come.

The person held in the arms of pleasure makes tomorrow his convenient time for salvation. But tomorrow comes, always in the form of today, yet he is never ready for that one essential step.

One thing is sure. Tomorrow will hold only that which we have prepared for today.

THE CHURCH I LIKE

I like a church with open arms
  Outstretched before a weary world,
Consoling those whom circumstance
  Upon life's bed of thorns has hurled.

I like a church that is sincere,
  Unmindful of the critic's voice;
For never will the church prevail
  That makes a wrong or lesser choice.

I like a church that loves mankind
  And ministers to every need;
For such a church commands respect;
  Its voice no one will fail to heed.

I like a church that preaches Christ
  And holds before the world His cross;
For never will that church decay
  Or through the ages suffer loss.

I like a church where I can feel
  At home, and with sincerity,
Enjoy the bracing fellowship
  Of Christian hospitality.

Thus as I try so haltingly
  To sketch the church that I like best,
I wonder if my church can pass
  With highest honors Heaven's test?

THIS IS THE CHURCH

The church I like must possess a vision. It must forget the difficulties through which it is now passing, and remember that it lives to bless the future as well as "to serve the present age." When our vision dims we begin to perish spiritually. The church is no exception. The short, present day view might temporarily bridge an emergency, but it can never provide strength for the days ahead. Perhaps a companion hymn is needed suggesting the thought that we minister to serve the future ages as well as the present day. This requires vision.

The church I like must possess a social passion. It must seek to save this and every age from corrupting influences that touch every area of life. It cannot preach, then turn its back upon industrial ills or national sins. It can never rest until war and the forces that create war are annihilated. These are not popular words at the moment of this writing. The church will not be popular if it stands firm in this conviction. Yet such a church is the only hope for a sane and well balanced world of the future. We cannot pray for a better world order and do nothing about backing up our prayers.

The church I like must never forget its mission. Its mission is to seek and save the lost. That includes men lost in poverty and nations lost in the ruins of war's destruction as well as lost humanity. However, I make reference now to lost individuals. The moment the church neglects the central theme of Christianity, salvation through Christ, it begins to die. Christ is the only hope for sinful humanity and the church is the only medium through which that gospel can be effectively preached.

WHAT OUR CHURCH SHOULD BE

*Our church should be a friendly place,
Where men from every class or race
Would feel at home, and know that they
Were welcomed in a Christ-like way.*

*Our church should be God's dwelling place,
Revealing to the world His grace;
Where souls would feel increasingly
The challenge of eternity.*

*Our church should be a hallowed place,
Above the mean things that debase;
Where from its pulpit would be heard
The vital message of God's word.*

*Our church should be a living place,
Yet doing nothing to disgrace
Through worldliness, its sacred name,
Lest it become a dying flame.*

*Our church should be a cleansing place,
Restoring peace, dark sins erase;
That builds anew when faith has waned;
Where blasted hopes can be regained.*

DOES YOUR CHURCH MIND ITS BUSINESS?

If it doesn't there is something wrong. The world in every age has said to the church, "Mind your own business." These words have been hurled by politics, the citadel of unrighteousness, sinful individuals and multitudes who have called themselves Christians. I now add my voice and say, "You're right." The church should mind its own business. I differ, however, in my interpretation of what that business is.

The Master left to the church a great deal of business to take care of or mind. The church that minds its own business is the church that faithfully does what the Master requires. This is sufficient to turn the world upside down and have accusing fingers constantly leveled in its direction.

The business of the church is to inaugurate moral reform. If it does that it will hear from every person engaged in immoral pursuits. The church stands opposed to any legislation that makes unrighteousness easier. It stands for every law that makes for a cleaner world. In this it cannot escape the shaking finger of politics. The church must labor to raise the living standards of all. Unscrupulous men will offer their condemnation when this begins to interfere with their profits.

The business of the church is to make sin unpopular. If it does not mind its business in this respect it represents weakness instead of strength. The church must not retreat!

If we were to sum up the accusation hurled at Jesus by His enemies it would amount to this, "Jesus of Nazareth mind your own business!" He was doing just that. He was minding the business His Father had entrusted to His care. He did not stop. They answered His aggressiveness with a cross. Can His church do less even when faced with a cross?

MY CHURCH

My church to me means life;
The more abundant life, enlarged, full-grown;
Unchanging in a swiftly moving age
When hope has flown.

My church to me means love;
An all-embracing love, secure, serene,
With hands outstretched to help the passing throng;
With self unseen.

My church to me means rest;
A quiet, peaceful rest, calm and complete;
Unbroken by the din of worldly strife;
The soul's retreat.

My church to me means home;
A happy, cheerful home, within whose walls
An undivided circle kneels in prayer,
As evening falls.

My church to me means God;
An understanding God who loves His own;
Who woos the sinful and consoles the saint,
When tempest blown.

My church to me means Christ;
A sympathetic Christ, with boundless love,
Who will not rest until each wayward child
Is safe above.

My church to me means hope;
A never failing hope when night descends,
For in that hour it lights the evening lamp
And comfort sends.

My church to me means faith;
Triumphant faith, that clears the cluttered way
Toward that city where for us awaits
Eternal day.

IF HE SHOULD COME

If Jesus should come to our church! Much has been written and preached on this subject, but has it become a part of your meditation? If so, perhaps you asked some of the following questions.

Would He be welcomed? If we invited Him to be our morning preacher and in the language of this day He preached that which so stirred the people of His time — what then? Would we welcome Him in our pulpit the second time? What if we welcomed Him to an Official Board meeting and He stood at the close to tell us how unwilling we were to put into practice the total program of the church? Would we snub Him the next time? Would our young people welcome Him? He would not be a kill-joy, yet He would not lightly pass over the sins of youth. And youth can sin. Would the older people welcome Him? "Yes," they would answer. Yet have we forgotten that He condemned more older folk of His day than He did youth?

Would He be understood? He was not understood in His day. Would the reverse be true now? Jesus would oppose much that men and nations sanction. What is done with those who persist in their opposition in Germany, Italy, Russia, America? Could Jesus escape the same fate?

Would He be happy? We have suggested that we might not be. What about Him? Would He approve the pagan means the church employs to support His ministers here and His missionaries abroad? Would He be conscious that He was in His Father's House?

If Christ should come! May we open our eyes! The Master is here! We might be blind but He sees and understands. He has taken the measure of our church.

TO SEE THE END

The Rock — that great soul Jesus carved
From common clay, with vision rare,
With others sat to see the end,
Enfeebled by his own despair.

He sat within the High Priest's court
And heard the rabble curse Christ's name,
Yet fear so gripped his tortured mind
He lied, denied, then wept for shame.

A weakened faith; a blasted hope,
Are twins that conquer men of might,
Distort their view; make small things great,
With nothing but the end in sight.

And down the ages men have felt
That Christ could not survive their day,
As Peter did that darkened night
When Christ was bound and led away.

Their souls have drooped in deep despair
While over all reigned one dread fear,
Which found its voice in these cold words,
"It is the end, the end is here!"

One lesson Peter learned that night,
A truth that then seemed far away,
That Christ must first be crucified
'Ere there could be an Easter day.

HOW BIG IS OUR FAITH

Have we not many times, like Peter, looked with aching heart and dimned vision upon what we believe certain to be the end? For over a year we have held in our unsteady hand the pen that is about to write "finis" to our civilization. We have freely predicted that Christianity could not outlive the vicious thrusts of a handful of small tyrants. In this we have reduced both Christianity and civilization and made them smaller than the power of a few godless men. We minimize the strength of God and the onward sweep of Christ and magnify the littleness of man.

Perhaps this chapter in the life of Peter can reveal our own pessimistic attitude. Peter's faith was buoyant when Jesus was able to continue His ministry without serious interruption. It was a fair-weather faith. But when the unexpected happened his faith waned. He walked with Jesus but failed to make the most of those three golden years. Is it not true that our faith glows when peace and prosperity reigns? But how big is our faith when the unexpected happens? Like Peter we see, not a glorious future, but only the end of all. A fair-weather faith will never stand the storms that continually arise. It is a sign that we, too, have not made the most of our Christian discipleship.

Again, Peter listened to Jesus, but did not take seriously what He said. Jesus was now facing the very crisis that He had warned would happen. Could it be possible that Peter believed all else Jesus said, but not this? Maybe not. But what of us? A fair-weather faith is only a sunshine faith. What we need is a faith that can master the storms.

AT THE CROSS

Hatred! Oh basest of all words;
Hatred made merry at Thy cross;
With crafty, fiendish glee it put
Its diabolic scheme across.

Indifference! That cold-blooded beast
Bereft of life and passionless;
Yet every nail that pierced Thy cross
Indifference hammered through Thy flesh.

Envy! Base demon of the heart,
Embedded in His cross we see
Thy name — it cannot be erased,
"For envy they delivered Thee."

But wait! How do we stand today?
Thou knoweth, Lord, for Thou cans't see;
Are we still driving nails of hate,
Or have we given ourselves to Thee?

HOW DO WE LOOK AT THE CROSS?

Have you tried to visualize the multitude at the foot of the cross? If so what have you seen? Is it compassion? Do you see a desire to intercede, even at this late hour, in His behalf? Or do you see a gathering of people who possess the characteristics of the mob? A few of the groups revealed through Scripture are as follows:

1. Those incapable of recognizing true values. Before them was an unsurpassed opportunity. Salvation could have been theirs that moment. However, as in the past, they continued to make nothing of that great opportunity.

2. Those whose interest centered in seeing a show. "Sitting down they watched Him there. They were ready. They had made themselves comfortable. Let the show begin. Is there a lesson here for Christians who support the Sunday evening movies?

3. Those who spend their time in childish play. The soldiers enjoyed themselves gambling at His feet. While He prayed they played. While He suffered they amused themselves. Would the Sunday golfer or pleasure devotee recognize himself as a part of this group?

4. Those who were more sensual than the rest. They railed upon Him. They taunted Him. They cursed. They told coarse jokes. They represent the sinful in the presence of the sinless. God only knows how many would be included in this group today. They include every individual in all lands engaged in war or any business that tends to destroy the onward progress of Christ's Kingdom.

However, this scene at the foot of the cross was not the end. A crucifixion never is. There follows an accounting, a judgment. The way we look at the cross determines every hour that follows.

HIS CROSS — MY CROSS

His cross was heavy, awkward, large,
  So very plain;
Designed to cause the utmost sense
  Of human pain.

My cross is made of yellow gold,
  A pretty thing;
I wear it, yet it has no weight,
  Or painful sting.

His cross bloomed from the blood-sweat of
  Gethsemane,
And bore salvation through the heat
  Of Calvary.

My Cross has never felt the drip
  Of blood and sweat,
And not through choice or force has it
  And Calvary met.

His cross still sheds upon the world
  A deathless glow;
My cross just dangles from a chain,
  Exposed for show.

OUR CROSS

This poem is not a criticism of the cross we carry in our processions, place upon our altars or wear. The cross stands for the very heart of our religion. It was written as a protest against the abuse surrounding our use or misuse of a symbol so sacred. We have made the wearing of the cross too common. It has become a popular piece of jewelry and often carries with it little significance. This was brought to my attention some time ago, when in a prominent place on our newspaper appeared the picture of two young women, arrested for the most revolting crimes. Yet dangling down the neck of each was a cross.

It reminded me of the oft repeated story of the school inspector who upon visiting a school gave a talk to the children on patriotism. As he proceeded he pointed to the American flag on the wall and asked, "What is that flag hanging there for?" One of the boys arose and said, "To hide the dirt, sir." Is it not true that there are individuals who wear this sacred emblem to hide the dirt, the filth, the sin that is in their lives? The cross is not to cover up sin. It is to reveal it and blot it from our lives. It is possible to wear a cross night and day, kneel before it and even kiss it, yet continue to be the same sinner.

I wear a cross. I shall continue to do so. I would want you to do the same. But my conscience will be ill at ease until I measure up to its standards.

However, we are expected to do more than wear a cross. We are to take up the cross and follow Him.

THE REPENTANCE OF PETER

*Without the High Priest's Court with aching heart,
His sturdy shoulders bent, eyes wet with tears,
The man that once his Lord had called a rock,
Is seen alone in prayer as daylight nears.*

*The night before within an upper room,
In vibrant tones was heard the boastful cry,
That though all others should forsake their Lord,
He would not flee, be faithless or deny.*

*He felt so sure that he would not succumb
To sins his Master had in sorrow bared;
His trust was all in self and not in Christ;
He faced life's greatest crisis unprepared.*

*How easy when within an upper room
Securely closeted with loyal friends,
To lightly view the hours yet unmet,
Alone, where Satan reigns, when night descends!*

*Yet 'ere the next few hours ticked away,
As evening shadows fled the coming light,
That boastful soul had thrice denied his Lord,
And transferred to his heart the pall of night.*

*His faithless act, his Master's look of love,
Revealed at last the man that lived within:
For years his vision scanned the world and self,
But did not pierce the realm of harbored sin.*

*With pride subdued and boastful spirit gone,
He slowly knelt and prayed in agony;
Thus changing common soil to holy ground,
And making it his own Gethsemane.*

*And now as sunlight hails the coming day,
In his repenting heart a fairer morn,
Unseen by human eye steals o'er his soul
And in its blaze of light a saint is born.*

HE DID IT!

Peter will always be loved. His weakness will, in a large measure, be overlooked. He is loved, because in his life with its many unsteady hours, we see a picture of ourselves. What a consolation it is, when we spiritually fail, to realize how precious he was in the sight of the Lord! The greatness of the man far overshadows his imperfections. It is refreshing to think, that in spite of our occasional mis-steps, perhaps our total life looms larger to the eyes of Jesus than our weakness.

One of the greatest things Peter did was to weep bitter tears of repentance after his base denial. This is not easy. He could have gone the way of Judas. He might easily have become an unbeliever. These are the ways of least resistance. They are the coward's way out of an unpleasant experience. Peter walked from the Courtyard the hard way. He faced the raging storm within with rare courage. In conquering this he conquered himself.

Peter has been labeled, and rightly so, for the hours preceding his repentance. We must, however, stop there. We have criticized him for the companions he chose that evening. They were not his companions. He repudiated them a few hours after they were made. We have bemoaned his tendency to compromise, but no compromise was made while on his knees. We condemn him for his boastfulness. Yet he did not boast in the midst of his shed tears. We have called him a coward. Yet he did the most manly and courageous thing demanded of any life.

How many of today's sinners are willing to follow his example? The world is full of cowardly men like Judas, but not enough heroic Peters.

BECAUSE CHRIST DIED

Because Christ died
A weeping world rejoiceth;
His cross has been a symbol and a guide,
And weary hearts have snapped their chains of bondage,
And found abundant life —
Because Christ died.

Because Christ died
The wall of death is broken;
The doors that time had raised He cast aside,
And those who live in Him have seen His Kingdom,
For Heaven starts on earth —
Because Christ died.

Because Christ died
Salvation has been offered;
No greater gift than this our Lord could give,
And through the ages men will tell with gladness,
How Jesus gave His life
That they might live.

HIS GIFT TO ME

Because Christ died I am no longer a pagan. My Anglo-Saxon ancestors ate human flesh and drank from human skulls. They were considered too hopeless mentally and morally to be the slaves of their captors. But this was all before Jesus gave His life upon the cross. At least it was before that message reached the pagan strongholds. But I today can rejoice that I am spared a pagan existence. The sacrifice of Christ has made the difference.

Because Christ died I possess a hope. It is the hope of salvation. If I face eternity with condemning sins upon my soul, I do it because I have repudiated Christ. The cross means salvation for me as well as for a sinful world. My hope rests in the fact that salvation is individual and personal.

Because Christ died I possess life. That life is in two parts. Part one is the life I now live. It is true that the most sinful and corrupt appear not only to be alive, but to enjoy their existence. Yet life is not a matter of meat, clothes, pleasure and bank accounts. Life is far deeper than this. It is something that vibrates within. It is not taken from the world, but given through Christ. This they do not possess. Hence they exist but do not live. Part two is the life I will eventually live. It is life everlasting. The life I now live and the life to come have been made possible because Christ died. This is His gift to me, to you and the whole world.

THE REMORSE OF JUDAS

*"What have I done, Oh Lord, what have I done!
How little did I think awhile ago
When talking with those crafty Pharisees,
That I so soon would drink this cup of woe!*

*It all seemed simple then—an easy thing,
To place you in their hands, and then to flee,
My heart was stung with hate, my eyes were blind,
I could not see that doom awaited me.*

*I thought of naught but self and wounded pride,
I craved for place, I yearned for gleaming gold,
Alas, how costly has that bargain proved —
It was not you, it was myself I sold!*

*And now forsaken by both God and man,
Alone with sins I must forever face,
I think of days when peace dwelt in my heart
And know that now remorse sits in its place.*

*A vulture swoops from out the darkened sky,
My nerve is gone, I struggle hard for breath,
I thought that what I did would bring me life,
And now, too late, I know it brought but death!*

*Death! Death! Oh Lord, that awful word of doom
Keeps ever pounding on my wretched heart,
The swooping vulture catches up the strain
As if it knew that life and I must part!*

*What have I done, Oh Lord, what have I done!
If from myself I could forever hide;
But no, death only offers me that hope,
By morn yon vulture will be satisfied!"*

THE MAN WHO COULDN'T TAKE IT

Judas was a prodigal who came to himself too late. When the awakening did come he shouted, "I have betrayed innocent blood!" His life teaches us, that we do not have to enter the far country and there waste our life in riotous living, to be a prodigal. Like the elder brother, who was ever in the presence of his father, we too can be in the presence of Jesus yet sinfully and recklessly betray Him.

Judas was one of the twelve most fortunate men of history. How we envy him! Called by Jesus to be one of His inner circle! He shared everything with the Master but His purpose and passion. Yet he became a greater prodigal than the young man Jesus had spoken of in his presence not so long before.

His life reveals that we can walk in the midst of light, yet live in darkness. The Gospels remind us of the time when the fatal bargain with evil was made in these words, "And it was night." Judas could carry out his act of treachery in the night because he had grown used to darkness. It had reigned in his mind, heart and soul long before the shadows marked the beginning of that fateful evening.

Judas was the man who couldn't take it. While a disciple he was jealous. He couldn't take it when Jesus bestowed honors upon others. He couldn't take the hardships, poverty and discipline Jesus expected of His followers. He couldn't take it when Jesus used passive resistance when dealing with His enemies, or when He refused to use worldly means to advance His Kingdom. He couldn't take it when a cross appeared to ruin his ambition for power, fame and wealth. And now, after the deed had been done and the blood money thrown on the ground he couldn't take the consequence of his act.

THE END THAT NEVER CAME

When Christ was taken from the cross
The rabble cast a knowing glance,
"The end," they said, not dreaming that
"The end" but marked His great advance.

A guard was set against His tomb,
"His day is done," the leaders cried;
"No longer will He trouble us,"
But men and death the Lord defied.

"This is the end," the rulers jeered
As persecution cut in twain
The church that dared to follow Him;
Yet both the church and Christ remain.

Are we still waiting for the end
Expecting Jesus' power to wane?
Oh Master, ages, spread the news
That they who wait shall wait in vain!

WHAT PETER DID NOT SEE

Our Lenten meditations began with the picture of Peter sitting in the High Priest's palace to see the end. That end never came. Peter thought so, but what he saw was the prelude to a new and far reaching beginning.

It was a new beginning for Jesus. Easter followed and from that moment on the Master was not confined to either time or space.

It was a new beginning for the world. The darkness that had cloaked the world so long began to lift and light settled upon the horizon.

It was a new beginning for Peter and the disciples. "Go tell His disciples and Peter," were among the first words spoken on the morning of the resurrection. Those who came to see the end were to be the first to witness the beginning.

It was the beginning of power. That evening in the upper room He said, "As my Father hath sent me even so send I you. Receive ye the Holy Spirit."

It was the beginning of an unswerving loyalty and faith. To Thomas He uttered these words, "Because thou hast seen me, thou hast believed. Blessed are they who have not seen and yet have believed."

It was the beginning of a teaching, pastoral mission to all people of all ages. "Feed my sheep. Feed my lambs," were His words to Peter.

It was the beginning of a great missionary enterprise. The words for this are to be found in His great commission.

It was the beginning of His constant, uninterrupted, empowering presence. "Lo, I am with you always."

Peter did not see the end.

THE FIRST EASTER

Throughout the night with heavy heart I waited
To catch the first faint rays of coming dawn;
It seemed as though an age passed in the darkness,
An age from which all hope had fully gone.

Still vividly I saw beyond the garden
The three dark crosses stamped against the sky;
How could I help but feel that with His passing
Jehovah, God Himself, had passed us by!

Dawn came at last and with some friends I journeyed
To see once more our Saviour, but instead
An angel met us with this joyous message,
"The Lord is risen whom you mourn as dead!"

A moment passed. We stood there staring, speechless;
A moment only, yet in that short space
The world completely changed. Light swallowed darkness;
All nature joined to praise God's act of grace.

Gone now the grief, the bitter disappointments;
Gone are the fears that filled my troubled breast,
Like music falling softly from the heavens
Came inward peace that set my soul at rest.

Throughout the day I hastened with the tidings,
And as I talked men heard with bated breath,
How God had used the cross for our Salvation,
The resurrection, triumph over death.

CHRIST LIVES! DO YOU?

Two texts come to my mind today. The first is from the Gospel of Mark and has reference to Christ, "He is risen!" The second is from Colossions referring to His followers, "If ye then be risen with Christ, seek those things which are above." The first was spoken by an angel at the empty tomb who knew God's plan for His Son. The second, by the Apostle Paul, who knew the Master's plan for His followers. The first message gives the assurance that Christ lives. The second gives the assurance that we too shall live providing we are risen with Him.

A vast number of worshippers today will never catch the Easter meaning. One reason is that they have not prepared themselves to accept it. They have not followed Him over the road to Calvary during the Lenten season. He who has not shared His passion, is not prepared to appreciate or receive the thrilling, life-giving message of Easter. Another reason is, that they will make no preparation today to carry the Easter gospel and its Master with them as they leave their churches. Tomorrow will be proof that they did not witness Christ's resurrection today. They will go about their daily routine as though nothing happened the day before. Christ is just as real after Easter as on Easter. He is still the risen Redeemer. His obligations have not changed. He expects as much from His followers. In fact, we are judged more by what we do tomorrow than by what is so easy for us to do today.

Christ lives! That is the message of Easter. Of that we need no proof. Our question should not be "Is Christ alive?" but "Am I alive?" Of that we must make sure. We will know the answer if our supreme desire is to seek daily the things that are above.

Christ lives Do you?

EASTER THOUGHTS

Easter must be reclaimed.
Too long the world has missed the Easter glow,
Charmed by the glitter of a fashion show,
A dress parade; a gala holiday,
With church-bound manikins upon display.
The faith of Easter never will be caught
By making Christ a fleeting afterthought.

Easter must be redeemed
From revelry that marks the end of Lent,
And worshippers who yearly are content
To journey to God's house, and then forget
That Christ still lives when Easter's sun has set.
The vision fades; the power soon is lost,
If Easter does not lead to Pentecost.

Easter must be relived.
Where is the zeal that followed Easter's birth?
The faith that doomed the soulless gods of earth?
No shallow, lifeless spirit of repose
Prevailed that cloudless morn when Christ arose.
The Easter atmosphere cannot revive
A torpid faith that thinks itself alive.

EASTER ALOOFNESS

As Cleopas and his companion journeyed to Jerusalem in company with one whom they did not recognize, the stranger asked them why they were so sad. Cleopas answered, "Art thou only a stranger in Jerusalem, and hast not known the things which are come to pass there in these days?" The first part of this answer has been translated to read, "Art thou aloof in Jerusalem?" Aloof in Jerusalem! In the Holy City, yet not a part of it! Living where God is without sensing His presence!

Is not this the reason why Easter comes and goes, leaving the world but little better than it found it? The fault rests not with this day, but with us. We walk the Easter highway completely aloof from the events that have taken place. Aloof at Easter! Standing in the presence of the empty tomb, yet not fully realizing its significance! Looking upon life's greatest event, yet receiving our greatest thrill from dress parades! Listening to an Easter sermon in a crowded church, yet planning a whole year of churchless Sundays that stretch before! Hearing the anthem "Christ is Risen" as the sun rises in the early dawn, as a part of the multitude hurrying home to bed after a night spent in riotous living!

Aloof at Easter! Treating the most sacred of all days as though it were equal with the most uninteresting and drab in our experience! Is there any wonder that the world is full of bad blood that sends forth its poisons of war, injustice and unrighteousness? The need of the hour is, that the world and the individual, be inoculated with the new blood and the new life of Easter.

EASTER QUESTIONS

Was it for colored jelly beans,
Or ribband bunnies without breath,
That Jesus turned with steadfast face
Toward Jerusalem and death?

Did He have nothing more in mind
When scourged or doomed by jeering cries
Than hot-cross buns or fluffy chicks?
A garden, rolling eggs, a prize?

Was Calvary meant to pave the way
For business, home and club to think
In terms of pleasure, greed and self?
Of flowers, merchandise and drink?

Did Jesus talk of gay decked hats,
Or gaudy, stunning Easter clothes,
As reasons for His sacrifice
To those He met, when He arose?

How easy in a world of things
For even those who follow Him,
To magnify life's novelties
And let the Easter glow grow dim.

MORE EASTER QUESTIONS

This and the previous poem, are two more of the many in this volume, written as a protest against the unchristian attitude of Christian people. How tragic it is to feel compelled to include those, who insist they are Christian, in the above statement. Yet if you should ask any night club or tavern proprietor if his patrons during the Easter season were pagan or Christian, he would reply "Christian."

Will you allow me to continue these Easter questions? If Easter means life, how can we continue to walk the highway of death? Self-destruction is inevitable to those who do not sense the burst of Easter life. Their way is the way of license and death.

If Easter means victory, what right have we to live on the level of personal defeat? We are not happy, confident Christians. The spirit of despair and defeat is written all too often on our faces. We have difficulty controlling ourselves.

If Easter means a rebirth of spiritual power, why is it the world is held in the embrace of a spiritual lethargy? Even if it is true that a stronger and more vital Christianity will emerge from the present chaotic conditions of the world, are we to overlook the present? Something created it. Optimism should not blind us to present realities. I have a feeling that if this new Christian era is to be inaugurated, we had better get busy and launch it.

If Easter means triumph over death, why are we still afraid of God's plan for the future? Whenever a sermon is announced on the subject of Heaven, people begin to squirm. Easter is the only Sunday the majority will sit quietly and listen. All life is a preparation for something. Why should we be only mildly interested in our preparation for the greatest future of all? Perhaps we have been too interested in "things." Let us try Christ this Easter.

SINCE CHRIST AROSE

Since Christ arose
The grave has lost its terror;
We know that death no longer can dispose
Of life, which is not fleeting, but eternal,
Unlocking heaven's gate —
Since Christ arose.

Since Christ arose
He is the mighty victor,
Dispelling doubt and crushing earthly foes,
And thus to all is offered full salvation,
And strength for every task —
Since Christ arose.

Since Christ arose
A living faith is given;
The weary souls of men have found repose,
And threatening fears that long made dark life's pathway
Have fled before that morn
When Christ arose.

Since Christ arose
Undying love has conquered,
And like a silent stream, unending flows,
From out the yearning heart of God the Father,
Back to the throne of grace —
Since Christ arose.

WHAT WAS BORN AT EASTER?

This question is usually asked at Christmas. Yet without Easter the world never would have heard the word Christmas. Everything pertaining to His birth has been preserved, not because of Christmas, but because of Easter.

What was born at Easter? Everything that is cherished by the Christian. This morning as you listened to the church bells pealing forth their joyous message, you were reminded that it was not only a special day but a different day from the rest of the week. It was Sunday. Sunday was born at Easter. Shortly after, you entered a building that you call your church. What gave the Christian church its birth? Pentecost? No, Easter, for without Easter there would have been no Pentecost. During the service your minister read from a section of the Bible. It was the New Testament, and was written because of Easter. A short time later the sermon was preached. The theme was life everlasting. These and all else that we cherish most, have come to us because the cross did not end all.

What was born at Easter? Everything that makes life new to the Christian. Easter means the beginning of a new life. We must be born again. It enables us to understand our mission in life. It did that to the disciples. They were no longer disheartened. They went forth to save the world. It also enables us to understand ourselves.

What was born at Easter? A new understanding of Jesus. The disciples had heard His words, but Calvary made them forget. When Easter dawned they remembered. Easter gives meaning to the purpose for which He came. It reminds us that He is not lost to us or the world. He is the same Christ, with the same love, sympathetic understanding and power.

THE WORLD NEEDS MEN

The world needs men who love the truth
And hold ideals others spurn:
Who work to conquer social ills
And make mankind their great concern.
It pleads for men whose thoughts are right,
Who give the pure and noble wings;
For they alone can lift the race
From baser thoughts to which it clings.

The world needs men — men unafraid
To face the marching hordes of might;
With well trained mind and ready voice
To speak courageously for right.
It calls for men who walk with God:
Who make the cause of Christ their own,
And in this flippant, careless age,
All other lifeless gods, disown.

GOD, GIVE US MEN

The world needs men who live like men. Men are no longer boys. Boys are irresponsible. When one becomes a man, childish things are put away. Animal passions and desires should have no place in the makeup of a man. When men live like men, they will refuse to sanction anything that will degrade or harm another.

The world needs men who are honest. Honesty in business is one thing. It is essential, but a man's honesty must exceed this. He must be honest in his convictions. He must be honest in his attitude toward his fellowmen. He should always see the best even though the worst is, for the moment, in the limelight. He must be honest in his desire to help those less fortunate than he. Everyone would receive adequate pay if every man worked for a better industrial order.

The world needs men who will be an example for every boy in their community. Boys will be men. Boys invariably follow the leader. Their leader can be anyone from the community scapegoat to their next door neighbor. Their Dad is assumed to be their example. What a responsibility falls upon him! For the sake of every boy, every man should be a worthy person to follow.

The world needs men who are interested in the moral welfare of their community. Moral conditions are not normal in any town. Would it be fair to say that men are responsible for these conditions? Who operates the tavern? Who are the gambling promoters? Who casts the majority of votes to keep that which degrades? These are questions every man can answer.

The world needs men who support the church and champions all Kingdom causes. Because this is our great need, our prayer is, "God, give us men!"

GIVE ME A FRIEND

Give me a friend whose charity
Extends throughout his length of days,
But yet whose gifts, however large,
Are not for show or worldly praise.

Give me a friend whose honesty
I can respect and ever feel,
That whether wealth or honored name,
He would not covet, stain or steal.

Give me a friend whose willingness
To help another when in need,
Is not confined to lodge or home,
Or stopped by color, race or creed.

Give me a friend who joyously
Proclaims his faith in God and man;
Who lives a helpful Christian life,
And changes "can't" to read "I can.!"

This is the friend I like the most,
Unselfish, righteous, ever true;
Thus do I pause and ask myself
Am I the friend I seek of you?"

MAKE WAY FOR YOUR FRIENDS

Give me a friend who will be by my side in life's crucial hours. This is, after all, the supreme test of friendship. When the news first went through my two parishes that my wife was lingering between life and death at the Martha's Vineyard Hospital, friends from both churches opened their hearts and homes to Joanne and me. Among them are two whose thoughtfulness I cannot refrain from recording. The first is a Selectman of Chilmark. The second, janitor of the church at Oak Bluffs. This was the message of each, "If your wife needs a blood transfusion, call on me." These are friendships that count. Their names will not be forgotten, and this simple record is one way in which that desire will be kept.

Give me Jesus as my greatest friend. This meditation, if you can call it that, is being written on the eve of the most trying days I have yet faced. After four serious operations within nine months and the possibility of more, the future for my wife is dark indeed. With the usual anguish of mind and heaviness of heart, I am attempting to write. How successfully, I do not know. Yet in these hours I have not ceased talking with the greatest Friend that has ever come into my life. What tomorrow will bring forth, no man can tell. Of this, however, I am sure. Jesus will be by her side and He will give unto me strength and courage for one more day.

Oh, friend, whoever you are, wherever you are, whatever your burden — do not lose contact with the greatest Friend God ever sent to this world.

> *"What a friend we have in Jesus,*
> *All our sins and griefs to bear!*
> *What a privilege to carry*
> *Everything to God in prayer!"*

A MOTHER'S LOVE

If I but had the voice to move
The human heart by way of song;
I'd sing about a mother's love,
A love unselfish, patient, strong.

If I but had the gift to paint,
Upon my canvas there would grow
A mother, from whose face would shine
The radiant light of love aglow.

If God had given me the power
To write one book that all would read,
My theme would be a mother's love —
A theme transcending race and creed.

I cannot sing or paint or write,
But I can live from day to day
A righteous life — a Christ-like life,
And thus a mother's love repay.

HIS MOTHER'S GOD

He was a ragged, disheveled, repugnant individual. For the past few years he had wandered from one place to another, a common tramp. During the World War he was a soldier in the German army and was severely wounded. His wounds were hastily cared for by unskilled hands. After the war, not able to get the proper medical treatment in exhausted Germany, he worked his way to America. However, due to the intense pain always present, he spent the little money he had on dope and drink. The only time I ever saw him was at the Dover Street Rescue Mission in Boston. I was chairman of a Gospel Team from Boston University, and we were holding services there that evening. At the invitation he came forward and knelt for prayer. His body was covered with sores. Of all men, he was the most repulsive. He confessed that he did not believe in God and even when he faced death on the battlefield he held no hope for the future life. When he arose at the close of the altar service, his first words were, "I can face mother now for I have found her God." Whatever else he had forgotten, he still remembered his mother's love and her faith in God.

The love of a Christian mother is never forgotten even by her wayward children. In spite of the blight of sin and apparent callous indifference, that one tender spot always remains.

If God has blessed us with such a mother let us forever rejoice.

> *"Oh mother, when I think of thee,*
> *'Tis but a step to Calvary,*
> *Thy gentle hand upon my brow*
> *Is leading me to Jesus now."*

MOTHER

God could not be in every place
With loving hands to help erase
The teardrops from each baby's face,
And so He thought of mother.

He could not send us here alone
And leave us thus to fate unknown,
Without providing for His own
The outstretched arms of mother.

God could not watch us night and day
And kneel beside our crib to pray,
Or kiss our little aches away;
And so He sent us mother.

DO NOT FAIL HER

This is a meditation, not only for mothers, but for sons and daughters. Are you a success? If so, perhaps you have given credit to your teachers who have imparted their knowledge to you. They need every word of praise you can bestow. They have not failed you. Perhaps you feel it is due to the influence of friends. They have not failed you either. But have you ever thought of your mother? She had you upon her heart long before your friends had you upon their mind. She was your first teacher. Before you entered school, she taught you the ways of honesty and righteous living. Before you received your degree from college, she gave you something college could not give and the world could not take away. She has not failed you.

If the success of sons and daughters is, to a great extent, due to mothers who have not failed, it is likewise true that mothers have become famous through children who have not failed them. Many noble women would not have outlived their generation were it not for the fact that they produced outstanding world or religious leaders. They live through the influence and greatness of their children. Mothers become famous, when their children go forth to bring to the world, all the love, service, devotion and sacrifice that they, as mothers have brought to them. Mothers, however noble, are not destined to live through infamous children. They have been betrayed through offspring who have failed them.

Your mother has not failed you. Do not fail her.

MEMORIAL DAY

We meet today to honor those
  Who served their country best,
From battlefield and fireside,
  And now, in quiet, rest.

Safe home at last, our soldier dead
  Have found unending peace;
And we, the living, dare not rest
  'Til wars forever cease.

We mourn another unseen host
  Who waved a fond good-bye,
From fields of service where they kept
  Life's standards ever high.

We see them passing in review,
  Their names we call to mind;
The doctors, preachers, common folk,
  Who lived to serve mankind.

We mourn our loved ones, lost awhile
  From their accustomed place;
But memory weaves anew their lives
  For us this day to trace.

Thus do we offer silent prayer
  While decking each green mound.
And softly tread with reverent steps
  This tear-stained, hallowed ground.

THE FORWARD LOOK OF MEMORIAL DAY

The obvious meaning of Memorial Day is that we shall not forget. It is a day of memories. The usual custom is to deck the graves of our patriot dead, those who have served their country well in times of peace, and our own loved ones. This we should do. It would be our duty even if no stated time were set aside for this purpose. But this is not all the day means. If we stop here we are not true to our honored dead, ourselves, or our beloved land. Memorial Day should have a profound effect upon our lives and thought. Those who gave their lives did not do it that we might simply deck their graves. They died for a purpose, a principle, a cause. It is for us to continue what they began.

Memorial Day should develop a higher patriotism. Not that of wild flag waving on one hand and the breaking of our nation's laws on the other. Not the low patriotism that cries "100% American," then goes forth to destroy another's freedom. Patriotism is more than pious talk, flag waving or cheering. Rather is it living and working for the highest ideals of American life.

Memorial Day is a challenge. A challenge that does not come to us through the lips of today's orators, but from the graves of our dead. The graves that we deck are not silent. They speak. They remind us of what God expects of us and of this land that we profess to love.

On Memorial Day we take a forward look. Memories always carry us back to the past. But on this day the past warns us to look into the future and make certain that war shall not again visit us, and zealously work to conquer the sins that have so long conquered mankind.

I WONDER

I wonder if again this year
  When loved ones meet,
To deck the graves of those who hailed
  Life's last retreat, —
If men will raise a pious voice
  And plead for boys
For war to crush, as children would
  Their soldier toys?

I wonder if the god of war
  Will rule the day,
Through so-called patriots who love
  War's grim display?
Or if the men of Cloth who serve
  The Prince of Peace,
Will give the Judas kiss, and back
  War's vast increase?

I wonder if upon this day
  The fearful loss,
The agony, the blood, crushed limbs,
  That mark each cross,
Will be forgotten, as men praise
  War's atmosphere?
And will the lips of Christ be stilled
  Again this year?

I BELIEVE IN AMERICA FIRST

A few years ago, after reading Memorial Day speeches and addresses, delivered by political orators of all descriptions, I was amazed and shocked by many of the things said. Some glorified war. Others saw nothing wrong in or with America. Many were on a pure materialistic plane. The underlying thought was "America first." The poem, "I Wonder," was written almost a year later with the addresses of the past Memorial Day fresh in mind. That was before the present war placed a much needed check on flippant public utterances. I too believe in America first, but not as some of these orators preached it.

I believe in America first, not in material matters but in the development of the spiritual. If we place America first in this direction, the material will take care of itself.

I believe in America first, not in terms of bigness, but of high ideals. We are not suffering from the lack of huge business enterprises, but from the lack of lofty ideals.

I believe in America first, not in power, pride or disdain, but in sympathy, love and understanding. The world's test of progress is in outward power, and power leads to pride and pride to disdain. Over against this we have the test of God, "Not by might, but by My Spirit."

I believe in America right. I cannot believe in any nation, any more than I can any individual, that is wrong. To say, "My country right or wrong," is as immoral as to say, "Myself right or wrong." The duty of the Christian is to bring right in the place of wrong.

I am sure our patriot dead, if they could speak, would remind us that if we fail to place America first in these directions, we fail them.

WHEN THEY HAD PRAYED

"When they had prayed," so reads the simple story,
An upper room became God's dwelling place,
Where all were one in spirit, faith and purpose,
Without a thought of color, class or race.

"When they had prayed," their meeting place was shaken,
The force of which was soon to rock the world
And cause the pagan gods to fear, then crumble
When in their midst the Christian strength was hurled.

"When they had prayed," they gave of their possessions;
None thought the Lord's request to give, extreme;
But greater than their homes, their gold or silver
They gave themselves, the sacrifice supreme.

"When they had prayed," they preached the Word with boldness,
These men whose lips the Lord had touched with fire;
To lose themselves in service, this their mission;
To do their Master's will, their great desire.

"When they had prayed," Oh, glorious words of power,
Resound within God's templed halls today,
And shake mankind from self and cold indifference,
That Christ, through us, might lead the world His way

WHAT DO YOU EXPECT?

You prayed at least once yesterday. You will do the same today and every day. When you prayed yesterday did you expect anything to happen? Will you expect something to happen today? If you do you will not be disappointed. Something will happen—at least to you, to your faith, to the cause of Christ that you represent. Nothing happens, only to those who pray, yet feel that the results will be the same in the future as in the past. Even before they close their eyes they are sure their prayer will not accomplish much.

How different the results that follow this attitude of prayer, from that which followed prayer at Pentecost and the days that came after. They possessed the spirit of expectancy. They were sure something would happen. They were not disappointed. It did happen. If they looked at prayer as many of us do, perhaps Pentecost never would have occured. The Acts of the Apostles might never have been written. The early church might have died in its infancy.

Can it be possible that Christianity is suffering, not from the lack of prayers, but from the lack of expectancy in its prayer life? Have we lost faith in our one great source of strength and power? Jesus never neglected His prayer life, yet He was God's Son. If He was sure that His prayers would be heard and answered, what reason have we for doubt?

I do not think that God has suddenly placed an embargo on the products of prayer. It can still shake the world. It is now, as then, the prelude to power. It will cause us to preach the Word with boldness, make us gracious Christians and send us forth as flaming evangels. Prayer has not changed. What about us?

MY PRAYER

I do not ask that Thou wilt make
    My life a song;
I only ask that Thou wilt help
    Me conquer wrong.

I do not seek to understand
    Thy plan divine;
But only pray that all my plans
    Conform to Thine.

I do not ask that Thou wilt take
    Life's pain away;
I only ask for fortitude
    And strength to pray.

I do not hope to find in life
    Unending peace
But ask that I may feel each day
    My faith increase.

I do not ask that Thou wilt lift
    My heavy load,
Or clear what obstacles may form
    Along my road.

I do not long for earthly goods,
    Or worldly fame;
But pray that nothing I desire
    Be to my shame.

Thus, Lord, I pray that Thou wilt take
    My tired hand,
And when I falter by the way,
    Help me to stand.

I BELIEVE IN PRAYER

Early one morning, many years ago, a young man spending the winter sealing on the cold, bleak shores of the Labrador, left on what almost ended in his last trip. After hauling his boat over the ice for a considerable distance, he reached open water. It was then daylight. Soon he sighted a seal, raised his gun and fired. He had done this many times before, but on this occasion grew careless and the boat capsized. He was thrown in the icy waters far from habitation. But something was happening elsewhere. His Christian mother in Newfoundland, hundreds of miles away, awakened suddenly at that very moment. Feeling that her son was in danger, she dropped on her knees by her bed and prayed that God would save him.

As she prayed, another man walking over the snow and ice of Labrador, heard faint cries from the ocean. He listened, but convinced it was birds, decided to continue his journey. He was going in the opposite direction and had no time to lose. However, before he had taken many steps, something compelled him to turn and go in the direction of the cries. He did not want to, but he said later, "I felt that there was some unknown power leading me on." Finally he reached the open sea, saw the drowning man, and rescued him.

How was it that a mother, hundreds of miles away, knew that her son was in danger? And how could her prayers turn another, against his own will, from the direction which he was going to the open sea to rescue her son? I do not know, entirely. But this I do know. That Christian mother was my grandmother, her son was my father, and I preach the gospel today because God heard and answered her prayer.

I believe in prayer!

A PASTOR'S PRAYER

Within this swiftly moving world
I pause, and pray that I might give
Myself for life's forgotten men,
Whose only sin is that they live.
And let me serve where 'ere men slave
For meagre pay; and daily fight
For racial love, the poor, world peace,
With naught of self to dim my sight.

I pray for strength that I might raise
The sinful from their tomb of death;
And in the ghastly bones of greed
Provide the sinews, flesh and breath.
And may my vision never dim,
Or faith decrease in this tense hour;
That I might live and preach the Word
With courage, confidence and power.

FAITH MARCHES ON

At the close of a most trying day, as I was about to leave the hospital, a young man stopped me and inquired about my wife. He was a stranger to me and I informed him that there was nothing new or more encouraging. After some reassuring words, he left. I stayed for a few minutes to talk with her nurse. When I left, he was waiting for me outside. After telling me of encouraging signs Dr. Glenn had noted earlier that evening, he said, "Everyone on the Island is pulling for your wife, and don't forget that Chap you preach about every Sunday." These were electrifying words, not that I had forgotten, but because that young man in his own way, recognized the power that rested in Jesus. Faith in "that Chap" is not only needed in life's crisis hours, but it is a faith that marches on.

That faith has marched into saddened homes and hearts in all ages, and provided the strength and courage demanded. It has marched into the haunts of darkness and sin, leaving always behind it a deathless glow.

However, the best news is, that it is not something that happened in the past. It is still happening today and will continue tomorrow. That faith will march over battle-scarred nations. Christ and His program of peace will yet triumph. In Christ is life and power. Without Him there can only be chaos, destruction and death.

May I never forget the "Chap" whom I love and continually preach.

WHEN TO PRAY

Pray when your life grows weary,
    Your days become drab and drear,
For these are the days you need guidance,
    And prayer brings the Master near.

Pray if youth is upon you;
    Cease not if you're in your prime,
And dare not if age compels you
    To bow to the rush of time.

Pray when the morning sunshine
    Illumines your upturned face;
Pray when the shades of evening
    Hold you in their fond embrace.

Pray when your joy aboundeth,
    And happiness marks your way;
For it's not in the long night watches
    That Christ is lost, but the day.

Pray when the shadows deepen,
    When low hangs the pall of night,
And into your home death enters,
    To smother the flickering light.

So pray in the morn and the evening,
    Show God and the world you care,
And He who heareth in secret,
    Will quietly answer your prayer.

A PRAYING DOCTOR

Perhaps the greatest contribution I can make, by way of this meditation, is to center our attention upon a profession that we do not often consider from the angle of prayer. Yet doctors do pray. Here is the story of one who relies upon God as well as his own ability. He is Dr. Chester L. Glenn of Oak Bluffs. These words, spoken a few months ago, will stand as a fitting introduction, "I continually prayed for Elsie and was confident she would turn the 'dark corner.'"

As a youth, although still young, he wanted to be either a minister or a doctor. He sought the guidance of a minister, and that conversation helped to settle the matter. He studied medicine. However, the urge that nearly sent him into the ministry never left him. He reads his Bible. He prays for his patients. He is one of the most conscientious men of his profession. If we could bring the faithful family doctor of other years up to date, make him aggressive, efficient, using the most advanced methods, we would have Dr. Glenn.

A short time ago he was a speaker at our Neighborhood Convention. The Neighborhood Convention, as many other good things, is a Martha's Vineyard institution. It is an all day meeting of the Island Protestant churches each month. Sermons, addresses and lectures are delivered by ministers and laymen from on or off the Island. Dr. Glenn was given the general theme of Religion and medicine, yet gave an inspirational message that challenged all who listened. He quoted Scripture throughout, especially stressing the value of prayer and faith.

Doctors are religious. They do pray, and I am sure Dr. Glenn would rejoice if I included with him, Dr. Thurman Rose of the U. S. Marine Hospital, Vineyard Haven, Dr. John P. Jones, Wakefield, Rhode Island, Dr. Herbert D. Adams of the Lahey Clinic, Boston, and all others who share their faith.

WHO WANTS THE KINGDOM?

Who wants the Kingdom?
The world that strives by force to crush the weak?
What would dictators do or wicked say
If governed by the righteous and the meek?
They cry for lands and people to enslave,
But His is not the Kingdom that they seek.

Who wants the Kingdom?
The church that harbors feelings which divide
While preaching unity and brotherhood?
The Kingdom will no longer be denied
When seers of color preach where white men meet
And priest and prophet labor side by side.

Who wants the Kingdom?
Do we who ask for it each time we pray?
Would we unloose the grip of hate and greed?
Of passion, worldly ties, and then display
An all-consuming love for what He loved?
We would—sometime perhaps—but not today!

WELL, WHO DOES?

Does the world? Would it be happy if His Kingdom should come suddenly—let us say tomorrow? This would mean heaven on earth. Could a world, not interested in paying the price for a Heaven in the future, be expected to sponsor a heavenly program for the here and now?

Do the self-appointed saviours of the day desire it? They go forth to conquer. According to them, they uphold the only righteous cause, and all standing in their way are pagan hordes. What would happen to them and their "righteous cause" if the Kingdom should come?

Would business welcome it? If it did exploitation would be unknown. There would be no inadequate pay on one hand and fabulous salaries on the other. Business would conduct itself on the basis of the Golden Rule. In the face of this, would it yearn for the Kingdom?

What about labor? Our sympathies, for the most part, are with organized labor. Yet what sins it has committed in the name of justice! It has, by no means, used Kingdom methods to accomplish its ends. I had an opportunity to see it work a few years ago, when the C. I. O. came into town. It rushed in on wings of violence, and displayed an utterly unchristian spirit throughout its brief stay. We wonder what labor would do if the Kingdom should come.

What about us? The Kingdom would come in us as well as the world. This would allow no room for sinful desires. Would we be happy?

In the face of this, do we honestly want the Kingdom, or are we only mumbling words? Let us not forget, that when we pray for the Kingdom, we pray for its Christ, and we cannot have Him without accepting His way of life.

MY SIN

I glibly prayed, "Thy will be done,"
 Then went my way
Unmindful that I asked His will
 Be done today.
I talked to God but gave my ear
 To earth's demands,
I sought His aid, then placed control
 In worldly hands.

"Thy will be done on earth," I cried
 Quite fervently,
But closed my mind to thoughts that it
 First start in me.
Condemning sins that cursed mankind
 In pious tone,
I pleaded that they be destroyed,
 But not my own.

I placed the emphasis on "Thy"
 In ringing speech,
Then moved that which I loved and served
 Beyond His reach.
And still I pray that earth might feel
 The will divine,
But still reserve the right to mold
 His will to mine.

THE SIN OF THE MULTITUDE

My sin is the sin of the multitude. I pray this petition with greater fervor than I practise it. For that reason it might be well for us to clarify our thinking on God's will versus man's will.

Failure to distinguish between the will of God and the will of man, very often makes God responsible for everything. The destructiveness, the imperfections, the failures of man that lead to unnecessary sorrow and death, are all too often considered as the will of God. God does not will that men should die through war or become slaves of unrighteousness.

God cannot do His will alone. We must make it our will to do His will. He must have an opportunity to work out His will through us.

To do God's will is to lend dignity to all life. The lack of dignity in life is the result of man's will. Life becomes dignified only when it conducts itself in a dignified manner. Do we think of dignity when we think of bombs tearing mothers and babes apart? Do we think of dignity when we think in terms of moral baseness, sexual indecencies, drunkenness, attended by its mental paralysis on one hand, and its filth on the other? These debase, and only the will of God can dignify life.

The present condition of the world indicates that we have been going in the wrong direction. This has produced wrong results. The will of God gives the right direction to life.

How is God's will expressed? How are we to know? The answer can be given in two words, "through Jesus." Jesus came to make the will of God clear and understandable. To follow Him is to do God's will.

OUR MASTER

*Our Master was a man of faith
Who saw life's best, and pleadingly,
With thoughts away from sin and self,
He bids us see.*

*Our Master was a man of prayer,
Thus gaining strength from day to day;
And lest perchance our strength should wane,
He bids us pray.*

*Our Master was the dark world's light,
Symbolic of the life divine;
And lest our light should slowly dim,
He bids us shine.*

*Our Master stilled the stormy waves,
And caused the boisterous winds to cease;
And to our soul when tempest tossed,
He whispers peace.*

*Our Master gladly gave His life,
Salvation's fullness to bestow;
And with the gospel's saving power,
He bids us go.*

A COLORED CHRIST

Above the altar of the Bradley Memorial Baptist Church in Oak Bluffs, hangs a large painting of Jesus. The artist was Lewis A. Dominis, a young man and member of the church, the work being done in 1923. It is a picture of Christ with arms outstretched, for them. Above the painting appear these words, "Peace be to this House." This, however, is not the unusual feature. That which is unusual is the Master's face. It is not the face that we are accustomed to look upon. It is the face of a colored man. A colored Christ, with broad negro nose and dark skin. He looks down upon one of His most faithful servants, the Rev. Oscar E. Denniston, who has loyally served this church for forty years, as though bestowing upon him a special blessing. Every worshipper feels that this Christ is one with them, one in spirit, understanding and sympathy.

I frankly confess that when I first saw it I was a little startled, but after viewing it through the life and experience of these good people, I feel that way no longer. For is He not our Master? And the word "our" includes all men of all races.

I wonder how many of us ever see Christ as a Jew? I imagine that the picture we paint and hang above the altar of our own heart, is that of a Christ of our own race, color and social class.

Thank God our Master had a heart large enough to love the whole human race, a sympathy broad enough to embrace every soul, and a power great enough to draw all men to Him.

IN CHRIST

As bells in the evening pealing
    Their melodies strangely sweet,
Comes softly the words eternal,
    "In Christ" is the life complete.
And races living in darkness,
    Removed from the Gospel light,
Still hear, then quietly bury,
    Their soulless gods of the night.

Above the noise and confusion,
    The race for power and fame,
Amidst the sin and indifference,
    Is echoed the Master's name.
And even a world defiant,
    Where godless men blindly grope,
Has failed to silence the message,
    "In Christ" is the only hope.

And over fast graying nations
    Where ruthless conquerors meet,
Is heard through the din of battle
    "In Christ" is the life complete.
And soon the slaves and the vanquished,
    Grown weary of blood and strife,
Will rise and conquer their tyrants,
    And follow the Giver of life.

THE WORLD'S MOST TROUBLESOME RELIGION

Christianity always has been, still is, and ever will be the most troublesome religion in the world. This is because Jesus is the most troublesome personality. He so troubled the religious leaders of His day, that they concluded that the only way out was to get rid of Him. This they accomplished, only to find that He was far more troublesome after the crucifixion than He was before. They never lived down what they did. Their troubled conscience gave them no rest. Many of them suffered a death worse than His upon the cross.

There was another reason for their troubles. During His ministry they only had Him to contend with. His disciples merely followed His leadership. But after the resurrection, every follower of His became a troublesome person. Where ever the persecutors of the Lord went they found these trouble makers, who would not let them alone. Imprisonment and death only caused their number to multiply. Like their Master they continued to trouble unrighteous men and causes everywhere.

Christianity with its Christ, is still troubling the modern world, and as of old is doing it through His consecrated followers. It is troubling the strongholds of sin. Sin has no use for light. It lives and moves in darkness. But Christianity has an uncomfortable way of letting in light. It is troubling the sections of the world that glory in many gods and revel in witchcraft and superstition. It is troubling men and nations who glorify war. They are conscious of the handwriting upon the wall.

Thank God for this troublesome religion! It is the hope of the world. It is the only force that can save civilization.

OUR MONEY

It is not what we earn that makes us rich
  As riches are really known,
But how honest we are as we lay our hand
  On that which we call our own.

It is not what we keep that gives us peace
  In an age when peace is rare,
But how truthful we are as we lay aside
  Our own and the Master's share.

It is not what we spend that brings us joy,
  For death can be bought with gold,
But how certain we are when the price is paid
  That it's not ourselves we've sold.

So it's not what we earn or keep or spend
  That gives us an honest glow,
But how righteous we are in the face of each
  When only our God will know.

WHAT IS WORTH WHILE?

I know of no place where our money will accomplish more or do more good than in the field of religion. Whenever we give to the church, not only our money, but we also begin to work. We work through that which we give. We become local church workers. Not only do we pay our bills, but we minister to the children and youth in our Sunday School and young people's department. We become Home missionaries. We are indicating that we desire a better community, a more Christian America. We become foreign missionaries. We are anxious for the salvation of the world. In a very definite way we carry out the Great Commission, by making it possible for others to do that which we cannot do.

We will never know, in this life, the blessings brought to others through the use of our money. Perhaps the money we gave has been the means of saving some soul. Maybe it has made possible the conversion of whole families in the foreign field. It might have saved the life of some mother and baby in a Missionary hospital, or afforded a free bed in one of our church hospitals in America. Perhaps it has been responsible for sending some young man in the Christian Ministry, or young woman in one of the many branches of Christian service. This we will not know now. There is, however, one thing we do know, that when through the ministry of our church, comfort has been brought to those who mourn, guidance given to those in trouble, or someone blessed through the preaching of the Word, we through our unselfish giving have made it possible.

God has dealt bountifully with us. Our money is, after all, His money. May we deal as bountifully with Him.

TOGETHER

(For an aged couple)

Throughout these many changing years,
That brought both joy and sorrow's tears,
You shared life's burdens, griefs and fears,
Together.

You gained your strength by way of prayer,
And placed your lives in Jesus' care,
And scattered sunshine everywhere,
Together.

When o'er your home death's shadow fell,
And loved ones waved a fond farewell,
You trusted God, but bore it well,
Together.

Oh, dearest friends, your upturned face
Still makes this church a throne of grace,
As side by side you take your place,
Together.

How sweet must be the Lord's "Well done,"
For steadfast faith and victories won,
As now you face life's setting sun,
Together.

Together will you walk until
The Master calls, and at His will,
You'll change abodes but journey still,
Together.

WHOM GOD HATH JOINED TOGETHER

I can see them now, sitting in the front pew side by side, eyes always turned in the direction of the pulpit. Their names would be unknown outside of their circle of friends, yet they were as truly great in spirit as many who have been afforded a place among the world's choicest souls. Mr. and Mrs. William Crawshaw were born in England and raised in a religious atmosphere somewhat foreign to us of this modern day. He had been for years a Local Preacher, and in his country that meant the preparation and preaching of many sermons. Even after coming to the United States, he spent many years in City Mission work. He was never alone in his labors. His faithful wife was always by his side.

However, when I became their Pastor, they were walking the last mile of their earthly journey together. Then came an important anniversary and they were to celebrate it on Sunday. That week I wrote the poem, "Together," and read it at the morning service. They were together as usual, but unknown to them, it was to be their last. Mr. Crawshaw, who had been failing in health for sometime, left for another Home shortly after, preparing it for that day when both would walk together again.

God had once joined them together. They were never parted, not even by death. I have often contrasted their lives with names that are upon every tongue. Names that come from Hollywood and from leaders in all walks of life. Their main thought seems to be, not how to remain together, but how soon they can be legally parted. May we repeat over again, "Whom God hath joined together, let no man put asunder."

TOGETHER STILL

Together still!
In life you walked together;
You shared its warmth and bravely bore its chill;
And now within that Land of endless sunlight,
You journey side by side—
Together still.

Together still!
There is no painful labor
Where life is planned according to His will;
Your loom and kitchen offer untold pleasure,
As side by side you work—
Together still.

Together still!
Gone are life's lonely hours,
Yet as of old you'll scan each face until
That happy morn when loved ones travel homeward,
To journey by your side—
Together still.

WHEN SEPARATION IS IMPOSSIBLE

Several weeks after the preceding meditation was written, word was received that Mrs. Crawshaw had rejoined her husband. A short time later, members of the family requested a poem to be read at a radio memorial service for the couple, conducted by the Rev. John A. Swetnam. The poem, "Together Still," was the result. It is not included in this volume for its literary value, for it contains nothing of literary worth. It is offered only as a concluding chapter to the poem and meditation already presented.

Together still! Naturally! That which is given by God to hold us together here will not be relinquished there—at least not by Him. Sin separates us from both God and our fellowmen. Faithlessness leads to divorce. But separation is unknown to those who love God and walk together in this life.

God is love. Love not only unites, but as long as its power is not curtailed, it strongly cements. "Together" is a stronger word in Heaven because love is the foundation.

God is light. There can be no darkness where God dwells. "Eternal sunlight" or "endless day" are terms we use. Perhaps they are not entirely correct. Yet they express, however feeble, the light that must permeate Heaven.

God is a worker. Creation does not suggest idleness, and God is still creating. Our desire to think and work is a part of His plan. This desire to think, create, or to work at that which gives us enjoyment, will not end at the point we call death.

God is a yearning Father. We yearn for the footsteps of our loved ones. Heaven will not remove from a mother's or father's heart that which has followed them through life.

MISUNDERSTOOD

Not every flower that blooms is in a garden,
Nor hid among the brush of some far wood;
Before our eyes the purest grow unnoticed,
And die as they have lived—misunderstood.

Not every flower that blooms is void of beauty,
Nor lacking in its share of fragrant scent;
While Heaven is filled with rapture at its presence,
The world must crush it ere it be content.

Not every life is what the world acclaims it;
Not every soul is stained by selfish greed;
I've seen the flower that blooms alone, unnoticed,
Where others only saw a vicious weed.

Our lives are much the same as is the flower
That blooms amid life's ridicule and scorn;
We live our best today—the world tomorrow
Will seek to steal the virtue we have worn.

Although the world condemns, is her word final?
And does her charge of guilt prove that she's right?
Ah, many a flower has bloomed amidst her charges
Yet died unspotted in the Master's sight.

Then let us live our best what'ere confronts us;
A life that's pure need never blush for shame;
We sow in tears today, we reap tomorrow
Life's greatest gift to men—an honored name.

WHAT HURTS MOST?

What does hurt most? This question is almost impossible to answer, yet does it not take years to heal the wound caused from being misunderstood?

To be misunderstood is to be misjudged. Jesus said, "Judge not that ye be not judged." Why? Because we usually do not have in our possession all the facts, and we have no moral right to judge on the basis of what we do not know. This should cause us to withhold our opinions and still our tongue. Would it not be better to leave the judging process to God who has enough love, knowledge and mercy to deal justly and wisely?

We are not fair to others. We do not give them a "break." We seek not the good but the bad, and the more we dwell on one's badness the less of their goodness we will behold. We magnify that which we desire to loom big.

We are unfair to ourselves. We become small. Our souls shrivel. But above all, in exalting another's failure, we become blind to the many sins of our own life.

It is utterly unchristian and cruel. It places us on the same level with the cruel of all ages. Any unfair judgment is a cruel judgment. Many innocent graves have been dug in life's cemetery by the savage tongue of some fluttering, shallow, irresponsible person.

The Master condemns harsh, unsympathetic judgement. His disciples are to set a different example. They are to make lives happy and this cannot be done apart from an honest and sincere attempt at understanding.

Friend, if you are misunderstood, remember that Jesus has the last word!

POEMS

Great poets are born, not made, we say,
And our poems come the long, hard way,
So we miss the many through faulty sight
And read the few that our poets write;
But poems no human hand can pen
Arise each day from the lives of men.

A kindly deed and a cheery word;
A noble thought or a burden shared;
A mother's love and a babe's sweet smile;
A soul grown big in the face of trial;
These are lyrics unwritten, unsaid,
Gems of the soul that remain unread.

The poems that never will depart
Are found alone in the human heart,
And spring from laughter or blinding tears,
Becoming priceless with passing years,
Thus life sends forth its nuggets of gold,
Great poems that never will grow old.

POEMS OF POWER

Life is full of poems. We do not always distinguish them because of undeveloped eyesight. We do not hear them because we are more interested in the clattering noises of the world. We do not publish them because we lack the necessary love and Christian charity to give them wings.

Poems spring from the consciousness of one's sins. Every repenting soul gives expression to words that cause angels to rejoice. Perhaps we are unimpressed because we are not angels.

Poems are born in sorrow. Some of the most courageous words have come from the lips of those who knew that their days upon earth were few.

Poems arise from the strain and toil of labor. I remember a saint of God, broken in health from his years of toil, yet arising an hour earlier every morning that he might spend that period in uninterrupted devotion. His life, work, and ministry, was a continual poem.

Poems abound in every home. The uncomplaining mother, working early and late. The laughter of little children. The love and devotion of a Christian family. The daily altar that transforms a simple home into a sanctuary of God.

The poems written by human hand are few compared to those that greet us every day. We can all be poets if we think God's thoughts after Him. We can fill the world with love and beauty. But let us not forget that we must also be interpreters of the poems that surround us daily. These are poems of power.

GOD'S ANSWER

Before you came I built with care
  A world for you,
With mountains, ocean, rolling fields
  And skies of blue;
Yet now you walk where waving trees
  And flowers nod,
And say as only fools can say,
  "There is no God."

Before you came I fondly dreamed
  That with the years,
Your life would bring Me happiness
  Instead of tears.
I offered love, you asked instead
  A chastening rod,
And answered with each gift received,
  "There is no God."

Before you came I planned for you
  A fairer place
Then that which now your eyes behold,
  Or vision trace;
But scoffingly you hold that life
  Ends with the sod
Thus by your choice your path leads where
  There is no God.

GOD DOES SPEAK

God always has an answer, even for the foolishness of the fool. Although not audible, it is so real that everyone sometime or another hears it. For the children of God it comes like music, but the fool, hearing it, trembles.

God's answer is to be found in the world He has created. How often we sing, "This is my Father's world." We believe it in spite of the many who live as though it were their world. Anything that detracts from the beauty, harmony, and happiness that God intended, comes not through Him, but the wickedness of man.

God's answer is to be found in His greatest creation—man. No one can make man. They can unmake him, in the same manner a child can break the perfect mechanism of a watch. The nearest a human builder can approach the creation of man is by way of a mechanical toy. But God alone can breathe into man the breath of life.

God's answer is to be found in conscience. The still small voice continues to accuse. Conscience, however subdued, finds some opportunity in every life to arouse and condemn. God, unceasingly, answers the fool.

But God's answer comes in another way. It is sin that makes the fool. He doubts all else, because his sin makes him unhappy in the presence of God. To be consistent he must say there is no God in any realm. God answers at the root of one's sin. That answer came in the sending of His Son, not to prove that He exists in His creation, but to save the fool from his sin.

No matter how foolish we have been, God has an answer for us. We can rest assured that answer is based on love.

THE PRICE OF WAR

Debt is the price of war:
An overwhelming debt none can escape,
Impoverishing the purse, the mind, the soul,
By way of murder, treachery, and rape.

Hate is the price of war:
A hate that dwarfs the soul—holds love at bay,
Transforming kindly men to hardened brutes,
To skulk as beasts prepared to kill their prey.

Doubt is the price of war:
A doubt that laughs at God and scoffs at right,
Destroying that which only can give peace
To righteous, yearning hearts; the soul's swift blight

Death is the price of war:
A devastating death, direct and sure,
And with it death of every worth-while thing
That makes both life and happiness secure.

War is the price of war:
And some day men will learn what history proves—
That war but sows the seed from which will spring
A greater war; and to this end war moves.

MAN'S INHUMANITY TO MAN

On September 25, 1852, the whaleship Citizen of New Bedford, ran aground in the Arctic. Five men were lost. Captain Thomas Howes Norton and the remainder of his crew reached the shore with only the clothes they wore as protection against the bitter weather that already had begun. That winter was one of intense suffering. Although given shelter by friendly Eskimos, they faced starvation, for the natives did not have sufficient food for themselves. It was not until the last of June the following year that they were rescued.

This, however, is only a part of the story. On October 3, a week and a day after they were wrecked, a ship appeared not far from shore. It was another whaleship, also named Citizen, of Nantucket. The men upon the shore made every possible signal, but there was no response. It was later learned that the signals were seen and reported aboard the ship by the mate, who requested a boat to go to their relief. This the captain refused, and the ship passed down the coast and out of sight.

Almost a year later, Captain Norton had the following published in Chaplain Samuel C. Damon's Journal at Honolulu: "Through the inhumanity of Captain Bailey, we were compelled to remain nine months, in this barren region, destitute of clothing and food other than the natives could supply us from their scanty stores of blubber and furs. During this time two of the crew perished with cold, and left their bones to bleach among the snows of the north as a monument to 'man's inhumanity to man.' "

War, with its devastating blight, stands always as a monument to "man's inhumanity to man."

ARMISTICE DAY

How well this age recalls your timely birth,
When human vultures stalked a blood-soaked earth;
No ancient hero passing in review
Received the wild acclaim accorded you;
And we, resenting not the love you bore,
Proclaimed with zeal that war would be no more.

Since then the fleeting years have come and gone,
Erasing gory scenes you looked upon;
Yet earth, still wet with blood from unhealed scars,
Again bends low before the god of Mars;
But this you taught—that war will never cease
Until men bow before the Prince of Peace.

WE ARE STILL SLAVES

Among the splendid works of art in Rockefeller Center, are four murals by Jose Maria Sert. They depict man's progress toward present day civilization, especially the eradicating of those forces that destroy life and happiness, and the evolution of that which has brought light, harmony, and contentment.

His four murals are a protrayal of the development of machinery, the eradication of disease, the suppression of war and the abolition of slavery. Strangely enough, the one that attracted my attention, was not the suppression of war but the abolition of slavery. It illustrates the steps of freedom from very earliest man, through the thousands of years of human slavery, down to the present hour. At the top of the picture men are seen still breaking the chains that bind, but the man at the very peak is carrying a cannon upon his back.

This Armistice Day reminds us, that in spite of our bid for freedom, we are still slaves. Slaves to the world's greatest curse—war. Even when this poem was written several years ago, conditions were grave. A few lines of it are now out of date. The proportions reached since then can only be described with difficulty.

For vast millions of people Armistice Day is but a memory. While their leaders cry "freedom" they know that they are but slaves. Slaves of a cruel institution that dates back to the very dawn of history. We abhor the wretched existence of the cave man, yet we hold to our breast the only method he knew of ridding himself of those forces bent on his destruction. Think of it! Twentieth Century Christians with cave-men thoughts concerning armed force!

TWO GODS

Before mankind, with outstretched arms
I stand and offer peace and life.
Men only look, then carelessly
Pass on their way. The air is rife
With groans of war; the world is mad;
Death's yawning precipice appears
And lures them on; its hungry mouth
Poised for the feast. Destruction nears.

I will not rest until wars cease;
For lo, I am the god of peace.

Before the world, with bloody hands,
I stand and offer unto youth,
Blind eyes, torn bodies, painful death,
Hatred for love; falsehood for truth.
I offer famine, rape and doom
To children, age and womanhood;
Yet multitudes obey my will,
And worship me and call me good.

I will not rest 'till all men die;
For lo, the god of war am I.

THE GODS SPEAK

Of all the gods in the universe, these are two that have been extremely active. The gods should work together, but in this case they are bitter enemies. Both seek to gain control of the mind, conscience and vote of mankind. The first god appeals to the best there is in man. It seeks his sympathies, understanding and love. The second god makes its appeal on the basis of man's animal instincts. It touches his brute passions. It stimulates his ego for pomp, position of authority, glory and medals. The first god offers happiness, hope, comfort and the right to follow the course planned for every life by God. It rejoices in the maintenance of beautiful buildings, comfortable homes, and above all, human life. The second god offers lawlessness, licentiousness, reckless daring, and everything pertaining to godlessness. It talks in terms of destruction that can go only one way, the way of the enemy. On that basis it teaches how to destroy and kill. It strongly approves the destruction of enemy buildings, hospitals and homes within range. It applauds the wanton slaughter of the innocent. These are the two gods that have always clashed. The first is the god of peace. The second the god of war.

Two gods! Each making the strongest bid for your support! What will your decision be? Which god will you follow? The god of peace stands for life. The god of war means death. You cannot follow both. Whatever your decision, remember the Master. We must eventually reckon with Him.

THE VOICE OF EUROPE

A nation's voice and trusting youth,
Sweet sounding words, devoid of truth;
A flag, a cheer, emotions stirred.
Loud cannons boom and bands are heard;
Parades and drills; the air is tense,
A nation's voice pleads for defense.

The trap is set, a nation waits,
Not long, youth rarely hesitates;
The line is formed, the strong, the brave
Mere boys to fill some far-off grave;
The trap is sprung; with quickened breath
A nation lures them to their death.

A nation's voice—deluded youth,
With glamour gone, beholds the truth;
The truth of war, and this their pay—
Blind eyes, legs gone, arms blown away;
Oh, God, what wanton sacrifice!
A nation wars—youth pays the price!

IT MUSN'T HAPPEN HERE!

How often have we looked upon our confused and unsteady world and wondered how Christ would ever be able to steady it again. In spite of faith's assurance that right will eventually triumph, we cannot help but visualize the destruction, to every area of life, that must inevitably follow in the wake of brute force. Paganism is on the march, and the fruits of its devastating blight is not confined to any one section of the globe. The nations have been brought so close together through man's inventive genius, that they resemble many families living in one large house. Only thin walls and frail doors separate. The disease that affects the occupants of one room, must by our very nearness affect in some measure, the whole house.

That there is a disease is apparent. For years certain nations have been gripped with a fever that has steadily mounted. Doctors of all descriptions have been consulted. They have but added to that fever. Some have prescribed seizure of lands belonging to defenseless or backward people. The rape of Ethiopia and the mutilation of the smaller and larger nations of Europe have resulted. Other doctors have sought to amputate democracy, producing Communism on one hand and Facism on the other, both systems leading to the same inevitable end—godlessness. Still other doctors have stressed the need of racial hatred, especially against the Jews. All of these prescriptions are based on violence and bloodshed, and the world staggers along with a steadily rising fever. Who will pay the price for these remedies? The doctors who prescribe them? Sadly enough, no. The price will be paid by youth and all who can ill afford it.

There's something wrong! This is it—of all the doctors consulted, never once has advice been secured from the only Physician who can heal—Jesus.

IF MEN MUST KILL

If men must kill—
Why should it not be lust for greed and power?
Not men, who know themselves but slaves
In that dread hour.

If men must kill—
Then kill the spirit to retaliate,
Instead of women, invalids and babes,
Victims of hate.

If men must kill—
Let it be that which favors war's increase,
Instead of faith in God and human kind,
Earth's source of peace.

ONWARD CHRISTIAN SOLDIERS

I abhor the word "kill" as it is commonly used and understood. Although applied to accidental deaths, it more often suggests murder. I did not, for this reason, like the words, "If Men Must Kill" as the title of the poem. However, I found it difficult to express what I had in mind in any other way, and now I must justify its use. But are we not as Christians called upon to rid the world of that which is unchristian? May we look at some of these undesirables in the light of Armistice Day.

War kills love. Christians are called upon to kill hate. Hate is the poison that keeps war alive. If love had its way, trumpets of peace would be sounding this moment instead of bugles calling men to destroy and kill.

War kills hope. We are to be crusaders against despair. Our duty is to drive from the world that which destroys hope, by keeping it alive. Hopelessness breeds despondency. Despondency makes life no longer worth living or else leads to godlessness, which makes righteousness unbearable.

War kills faith. We must slay doubt. God does not give orders on the battlefield. Human minds assume that responsibility. Jesus' voice goes unheeded. Faith has no chance to flourish.

War kills peace. It is the world's greatest murderer. It does not content itself with killing the body. It kills everything that is worth while.

Christians are called into battle too. That which war kills we are to foster. That which war fosters we are to kill.

THE FRUIT OF PEACE

Faith is the fruit of peace:
A faith that lifts its head above the haze
Of doubt and fear produced by crushing wars,
And with full trust in God sings forth His praise.

Love is the fruit of peace:
A perfect love that smiles upon mankind,
With eyes that see and hands that gently heal;
But war gives birth to hate, and hate is blind.

Joy is the fruit of peace:
Triumphant joy that gladdens each new day,
And as the sun that sends its brilliant light,
Heaps happiness and calm upon life's way.

Life is the fruit of peace:
The sacred flame that burns throughout the earth,
And can be smothered, not by men of might,
But only by the One who gave it birth.

Peace is the fruit of peace:
And in this solemn hour we reach above
And pray that God may help mankind to see
That lasting values come through peace and love.

MAN'S BID FOR PEACE

I would like to make one further reference to Jose Maria Sert's murals in Rockefeller Center, that we might view them in the light of war. The mural dealing with the evolution of machinery, shows the development from the days when all labor was done by hand, to the present hour when machinery plays such an important part. Yet, to what use have we put these instruments of man's brain and muscle in a world at war? Is it not to destroy or help in the process of destruction? That is the height of our mechanical achievements when war strikes.

The second mural depicts the saving of life through the great strides made by medical science. It shows man's earliest method, that of giving the little aid he knew, and then making the sick one comfortable until death intervened. There follows a series of medical discoveries on a road leading always upward. Yet, in a world at war, the very thing for which these benefactors of the race were willing to sacrifice their own lives, the saving of others, is forgotten. The pagan conception of mutilation triumphs over the Christian concept of salvation.

The mural concerning the abolition of slavery has already been described, signifying that in spite of our freedom, when war comes we are still slaves. The theme of the fourth mural is the suppression of war. As with the others, it starts with man's first bid for peace, in spite of the conflict raging about. In the center are two huge cannons. Emerging from one is the upper part of a human body, holding a baby in its outstretched arms, ready to dash it below. Men, however, are walking out on the cannon, seeking to save the babe before it can be destroyed. It is man's bid for peace.

THE BIBLE

*Within this Holy Book we see
    God's plan unfold;
And on each page are to be found
    Nuggets of gold.*

*Though life provides its choicest store
    Of worldly things;
How small they are compared with what
    Our Bible brings.*

*When sorrow lays upon our heart
    Its heavy hand,
This Book assures us that our God
    Doth understand.*

*Though crushed by sin, or tossed about
    By constant strife,
Its pages lead us to the One
    Who transforms life.*

*When death stalks through our home and leaves
    Its burden sore,
How blessed is its promise of
    Life evermore.*

*Oh, Word of Truth, within a world
    Possessed by greed,
Teach us to place our faith in God,
    And on thee feed.*

THE BIBLE FINDS US

In another meditation I described the fate of the whaleship Citizen and the suffering of her crew during the long Artic winter. I did not mention how rescue finally came. I left that for this poem. In a number of the Eskimo huts, Captain Norton found religious tracts sent through various channels by Missionaries. They contained nuggets of gold from the Word of God. The Captain gathered as many of these as he could and upon the margins wrote the story of his plight. He then wrapped them in furs for protection, and gave them to every Eskimo traveling South. At the end of their destination they were to give them to others traveling from that point southward, in the hope that they would reach some port or individual who could secure help.

Some of these tracts reached Indian Point and came to the attention of Captain Jernegan of the whaleship Niger and Captain Goosman of the Joseph Hayden, who were working their way north to be on the grounds when the whaling season started. Both ships immediately made their way through the floating ice to the point where Captain Norton and his men were marooned.

Thus did various portions of the Bible, that has brought life into the world, bring life to a group of half starved men who had spent nine torturous months in the frozen wastes of the Arctic.

We find the Bible, and in it we find life. But let us not forget that the Bible has a way of finding us. When we are lost, marooned on the frozen wastes of sin, if our eyes behold those sacred pages they will find and save us. The Bible gets us God and through it God gets us.

THE END OF THE DAY

The morning may greet us with courage and hope,
  And leave us with blessings untold;
And the hours of daylight may offer us joy,
  As slowly they start to unfold;
But nothing can lighten our burdensome load,
  Or gladden our troublesome way,
As the peace and contentment that wells in our heart,
  When we come to the end of the day.

When we come to the end of the day and think
  Of the sorrows that might have been,
Or the dangers that lurked, though unseen, by our side
  Where the crossroads of trouble begin.
It is then we remember our debt unto God,
  A debt we will never repay,
And the glory of Heaven illumines our home,
  When we come to the end of the day.

When we come to the end of the day and pause
  As we offer our evening prayer;
We cannot forget how sincere is God's love;
  How constant His fatherly care.
And we'll trust Him the more as we journey along,
  A trust He will never betray,
And our anthems of praise will resound through our home,
  When we come to the end of the day.

When we come to the end of the day of life,
  And prepare at last to depart;
No fear of the future will darken our road,
  No sadness will burden our heart.
But we'll gather our tools worn and battered through use,
  And quietly put them away,
And our rest will surpass even that we thought best,
  When we come to the end of each day.

THE END THAT DOES COME

The end of the day! Have you not thrilled at these words? Perhaps the persons seeking excitement have not caught their meaning. The end comes too soon for them, but not for the soul who has experienced the contentment the day's ending can bring.

The end of the day means the cessation of work. You have labored hard. Weariness has crept in upon you. Only a few minutes more and the tools can be laid aside. It is the end of the day, and your place of business will not see you again until tomorrow.

It means home. You have listened to disturbing noises from early morning. Problems, difficult situations, business worries have marked every hour. How refreshing at the end of the day to go home! Home means loved ones, and loved ones, happiness.

It means beauty. The day's end brings the golden sunset, the stars that twinkle and the moon that lights a path through the night. It is the beauty of harmony and peace.

It means rest. You are tired. Your nerves have been on edge throughout the day. You wonder how you can continue. But the end of the day ushers in the night, and night brings rest. In the morning you feel as new as the day you greet.

The end of the day suggests God's way of ending things. As it brings cessation of work, home, loved ones, beauty and rest to each life, we can be sure that when God provides an ending to our final day on earth, this and more will greet us.

IF WE BUT KNEW

Oh, friends, if we but sensed the thoughts
    Or knew the heart,
Of those we wound and by our act
    Cause tears to start;
We would not say the unkind things
    We often say,
Or seek to wrong the many souls
    That pass our way.

May we remember that each life
    Is much the same,
It matters not our place of birth,
    Our creed or name;
The word or deed that gives us pain
    Is felt by all,
And much we say that injures, pass
    Beyond recall.

We do not know but what that word
    May be our last,
And then too late will be our chance
    To change the past;
For life is short and those we wound
    May soon be gone,
And sad their going with our deed
    To think upon.

Oh, friends, may we be careful of
    Each word and act,
For only love that gives, can keep
    Friendship intact;
And that which we will cherish most
    Each passing day,
Will be the friends we kept, not lost,
    Along life's way.

THE PRODIGAL'S BROTHER

A classmate in college, Maurice Hodder, now a minister in Australia, once related to me this story. It was of a man he met aboard ship, who had spent twenty-five years shoveling coal in the stoke hole. His father had provided him with a good education, but being dissatisfied with the quiet of his home, he began to live a fast life. He finally did something that brought shame upon his family and broke the hearts of his parents. Shortly after he left home, but before he went his elder brother warned him never to return. Being ashamed of his sin, he decided to hide from the world as a fireman on a ship, rather than seek a business career for which he was trained. Ten years later he planned to go home to the parents he loved, seek their forgiveness, and start life anew.

He said, "There was a joy in my heart at seeing mother and father. When I reached the gate my heart beat faster. I knew they would forgive me. However, my elder brother was on the piazza and saw me coming. He ran down to where I was, pointed his finger at me, and said, 'Are you back? Didn't I tell you never to come again? Now get!' I was so discouraged and weak that I made no answer. I turned and walked out the gate, never seeing the ones I loved. I came back to my old job and that's why I'm still here."

The years have not erased that story. It seems as though I can see the elder brother as well as the prodigal. It has, however, turned attention to myself, causing me to ask, "Have I been an elder brother to someone else because I did not know?"

THE THINGS WE LEAVE UNDONE

We talk of the many things we do
    With an outward show of pride,
And tell how we gave a helping hand
    To those who walk by our side;
But the God who sees the hearts of men
    And knows the deeds of each one,
Remembers, together with what we do,
    The things that we leave undone.

There is much we do to merit praise,
    That will never be revealed;
And much we say to revive lost hope
    Will ever remain concealed;
But that which robs our lives of the best,
    Each day with the setting sun,
Is not alone in the things we do,
    But the things we leave undone.

The things that we leave undone are real,
    As real as the things we do,
And all too late are we forced to pray,
    "Oh, Lord, if I only knew!"
But God is good and His patience great,
    And He offers to each one,
A chance each day to faithfully do
    The things that remain undone.

TAKING OUR OWN MEASURE

The things that we leave undone are not only real, they are vital. They reveal what we are as truly as the things we do. In other words, our lives, character and religion are measured by the undone as well as by that which we do.

Our conduct is often responsible for that which we leave undone, and we are measured by our behavior. It is proper for us to seek every available means in developing our religious life on the Sabbath. However, the test comes, not on the basis of this one day, but the way in which we carry the Sunday spirit into the week. If we leave undone that which we promised to do through the channels of devotion, our lack of sincerity will be revealed in our conduct.

Our disposition causes us to leave many things undone, and we are measured by it. How attractive we can be at social functions! How agreeable and sweet when out in company! But we are not measured by this. Rather are we measured by the agreeable or disagreeable dispositions we take back to our homes, after the party has broken up or our friends of the evening have gone.

What we give to life reveals much that has been left undone. Dictators give war. The business man selling that which destroys, however legal, gives disease, poverty and death. Such lives are an indication, not only of what they give, but that they have left undone the finer Christian things that elevate and develop.

What we take from life points to that which is left undone. Life offers the easy and the hard, the pure and the vulgar, the low road and the high. What we accept reveals what we are.

IF WE BUT HAD A DAY

*If we but had a day to live
    We'd plan it well;
We'd light each moment with love's glow,
    And ere night fell,
Our friends would feel the healing touch
    Our hands had wrought,
And cherish long the quiet peace
    Our presence brought.*

*If we but had a day to live
    How kind we'd be,
And thoughtful, doing that which now
    We fail to see;
And somehow we'd find time before
    The setting sun,
To do the many worth while things
    We've left undone.*

*If we but had a day to live
    Our souls would reach
For God, and we would practice then
    What now we preach;
And Heaven, which throughout life's span
    Seemed far away,
Would rule our thoughts, if we could live
    But one more day.*

THE BIG TWO LETTER WORD

There are many "big" words in the dictionary. For the most part, we either stumble over or ignore them entirely. However, when we turn to the dictionary of life, we find that one of the biggest words has only two letters. It is the word "if." I will mention a few ways in which it is more commonly used.

"If we had our lives to live over again!" Especially have we said this when some blunder or tragic mistake has been made. If we could begin again what would we do? Would we recognize the value of time? Squandering time has been largely responsible for our present plight. Would we place more emphasis upon service? Our question has too long been, "What am I going to get out of life?" rather than "What can I give to it?" Would we give God the chance to do with us what we have refused Him thus far? These and other questions should be asked in connection with this "if."

"If we had luck!" Is this not used as a cloak to cover our lazy, indifferent, planless lives? The person who awaits the visit of lady luck usually spends and ends his life in poverty.

"If we had only known!" These words very often escape our lips when the results of our sins have been made known. It is the cry of anguish at being caught rather than repentance.

"If" is a word that spells tragedy, a tragedy shaped largely by our own hands.

If we but had a day, what would we do? Many things we never think of now. That day will eventually come, so why not begin now to prepare against any possible regrets.

TOO LATE

Tonight as I sit in my study
I ponder with sadness of heart,
The words from a life crushed by sorrow
That touched me and will not depart.

It happened today as I entered
A home that death's hand had made bare,
And stood in the midst of the mourners
To offer a comforting prayer.

The flowers were heaped on the casket,
And after the prayer had been said,
They gathered, surrounded by lilies,
To look once again on their dead.

'Twas then came the words full of meaning,
Words spoken in sorrow, not hate,
"They did not come near through dad's illness,
They sent him their flowers—to late!"

"Too late!" What a sad, dreary message!
How cruel its hollow refrain,
To torture the hearts torn by sorrow,
Increasing, not easing their pain.

I thought of how heedless and selfish
We are to our friends, small and great,
To walk past their door when they need us,
Then send them our flowers—too late!

THERE'S SOMETHING WRONG

The poem, "Too Late," was written at the close of a day known so well to every minister. That morning the telephone brought the message that a member of the church had passed away during the night. Shortly after, I entered the saddened home, offered a few words of consolation, and a prayer. As we stood before the casket, the widow, supported by her two children—splendid, well educated young people—the young man pointed at the mass of flowers. "These came too late," he said. "The majority of those who sent them did not come near during dad's long illness." No words he might have spoken could have expressed a greater tragedy than this.

"Too late!" Are not these the words that confront us continually? Not only do we send our flowers too late, but our words of praise also. In this, as every such case, the goodness of the man was openly discussed everywhere. But it was too late. These words should have come years before.

The tragedy of these words finds expression in other avenues of life. We meant to seek forgiveness from the one we injured, but we waited too long. We intended to write a letter to a friend we knew to be despondent, but we had so much else to do. The letter was never written. We planned to call on the sick, but our day's activity left no room. Our intentions were good as we faced numberless opportunities to be of service. Then the day came when our all but forgotten plans could no longer be fulfilled. We were too late, and our belated words sounded hollow, and our offers of assistance, soulless.

FORSAKEN

"Forsaken,"—sad indeed is life
    When we are thus bereft of friends,
And forced to tread the dismal vale,
    Where sorrows start and gladness ends.
'Tis then we learn with aching heart,
That death begins when friends depart.

"Forsaken,"—who can understand
    The tragedy this word reveals;
Or who can look within man's life
    To read the pain his soul conceals.
A fiendish mind alone conceives
The cruel wounds "forsaken" leaves.

"Forsaken,"—ah, but not by God!
    He does not thus forsake His own;
Though friends may fail, still rest assured
    With Him no life is left alone.
With self, "forsaken" means despair;
With God, new hopes loom everywhere.

WHAT'S THE USE

If Jesus had His way no one would be forsaken. Will you recall the story of the lost sheep. It might have been just another sheep to some shepherds, but not to the shepherd of this parable. To search for that sheep would mean loss of rest. The day had ended. Night had come, bringing with it the well deserved rest for the one who had labored through the heat of the day. Yet this lone sheep was more precious than sleep. It meant pain. The sheep was somewhere on the thorn-infested hills. The shepherd was aware that he would be cut and bruised in the darkness before it was found. But he was willing to face the pain rather than forsake the sheep.

Paul Laurence Dunbar in his poem, "The Little Black Sheep," tells the story in a most striking way. The shepherd asks the hireling to search for the lost sheep, but the hireling refused because the sheep was black and bad. So the shepherd went forth himself, searching as though this was the only one he owned. After finding and returning with it, the hireling frowned and said, "Don't bring that sheep to me." But the shepherd smiled and pressed it closer to his bosom. Paul Laurence Dunbar ends his poem with these words, "An'—dat lil' brack sheep——wuz—me!"

We might be forsaken by the hirelings of life, but never by the Good Shepherd. When we become disillusioned and cry, "What's the use," let us remember the One who does not know how to forget.

DO NOT GIVE UP

Do not give up, fellow Christian!
It's courage despondency needs,
And feet grown weary with travel,
Are watching where your pathway leads.

Do not give up though life's highway
Be strewn with the failures you've made;
Success does not come through reclining,
But starting once more, unafraid.

Do not give up when faith's altar
Is rocked by indifference and doubt;
The soul that is inwardly strengthened,
Can master assaults from without.

Do not give up when the sunshine
Departs from your earthly abode;
'Tis then that God sends His sunshine
To brighten the rest of your road.

Do not give up, fellow Christian!
Let nothing you fear hold you down;
Whatever your cross, remember,
A cross but precedes a crown.

WHAT'S THE DIFFERENCE

On January 6, 1846, the whaleship Columbia from New London, returning from Honolulu, was wrecked on a reef off Sydenham's Island. The island was a crescent of low sand, fifty miles long, populated by cruel, indolent natives. Although many of them succeeded in getting to the wreck, not one offered to assist the drowning men. They were interested only in seizing and dividing the plunder. After the whalemen managed to reach shore and their lives spared through promises that some ship would come and reward the natives with gifts, they were left without food and water to exist as best they could. As the days wore on, they lived on anything they found, including a dog which they devoured raw. Although a distress signal had been placed in a coconut tree, there seemed no hope.

Meanwhile, several hundred miles at sea, the whaleship Chandler Price, picked up a fragment of smashed whaleboat and a bundle of staves. This would have meant little to most captains, but to Captain John Hooper Pease of Edgartown, it meant a tragedy. He forgot about sperm whales, and ordered his ship about in a search of the islands for signs of life. For weeks he searched. Some of his men cursed the waste of time, but Captain Pease would repeat, "Finding that piece of whaleboat was a circumstance. That's what it was, a circumstance." Finally, on January 31, the Chandler Price approached Sydenham's Island and saw the signal of distress in the coconut tree. The man who would not give up, rescued the half-dead survivors of the Columbia.

"What's the difference," might be the cry of many, but not to the man who refuses to give up.

SHADOWS

Some shadows are dark and foreboding,
Like giants they hang o'er our way,
Though many are fleeting and distant,
Still others seem destined to stay.

For some it's the shadow of evil;
For others, the shadow of hate,
And drear is the pathway before us,
Where these darkened shadows await.

But not every shadow brings terror
To torture the wayfarer's heart;
For some are the shadows of healing,
That comfort us ere they depart.

God's peace is a shadow of healing,
And so is His shadow of love,
That touches our hearts, and with gladness,
We place our affections above.

And even the shadow of sorrow,
With death as its intimate friend,
Is only a shadow of healing,
That marks life's duration, not end.

Some shadows are dark and foreboding,
While others are cheery and bright;
Whatever our shadow, remember,
Behind every one is a light.

For shadows are not caused by darkness,
Though dark be their color from earth,
But either near by or in Heaven,
Some light gives each shadow its birth.

LIFE'S SHADOW HOURS

There are many things about shadows that impress us. One is that they do not spring from darkness. Shadows are possible only because somewhere there is a strong light.

Life has its shadow hours. Are we not aware that they must fall upon us all. Continual sunlight would not be good for our physical eyesight. It would be equally as bad for our spiritual sight. Our God, who was aware of this in the physical realm, did not forget in the realm of the spiritual. Thus, with the light of life, we must feel the effect of certain shadows. Sickness, disappointment, sorrow, death must take their place beside the minor shades more commonly experienced.

This we must ever bear in mind, shadows form only a small part of life's total span. They loom larger, because we have not accustomed ourselves to them, and the pain they leave cannot be removed in a few hours. Yet, let us not forget the light that is also present. The Psalmist saw it and exclaimed, "Even though I walk through the valley of the Shadow of death, I will fear no evil, for Thou art with me." He saw the Light that shone above the shadow of the valley.

We too cast shadows upon the world. Sometimes they take the form of uncertainty, doubt, indifference, selfishness, sin. But we can, if we will, cast healing shadows of faith, love, service, righteousness. Peter was able to cast a healing shadow because he was willing to pay the price for such power. His shadow was caused by a light stronger than the sun. It too was the light of a Son—the Son of God.

Perhaps the reason the shadows we cast are often dark, is because we do not stand in that Light.

THE WAY OF THE FATHER

We live in a world full of conflict,
  With evil arrayed against right;
But God does not leave us to perish,
  So precious are we in His sight.

Remember, when sadly neglected,
  And loneliness shadows our way,
That God is our constant companion,
  Forsaking us never a day.

And think when the cares of a lifetime
  Come slowly or cruelly swift;
That God would not burden our shoulders,
  If He stood not ready to lift.

Forget not, when evening decendeth,
  A warning of gathering night,
That He would not leave us in darkness
  Without holding for us some light.

Then smile when strong winds blow against us,
  Have faith in our Father above;
Remember, He never sends hardness,
  Without sending with it His love.

WHAT DOES GOD CARE?

Have you ever asked this question? Maybe you have not allowed the words to escape your lips, yet had them upon your thought. Well, what does God care?

God cares enough for His children to surround them with unlimited protection. Only an abnormal father has no interest in the welfare of his children. God has placed in His universe everything necessary for even the weakest child's protection.

God cares so much that He adds provision to protection. There must be ample food and adequate shelter. This He has unstintingly provided. Fruit and vegetables, fish of the sea, fowl of the air, animals that roam the earth—these are for our provision. In addition, He has given fertile fields to cultivate, and to make us warm and comfortable has placed in our midst, wood, oil, coal, rock and iron.

God cares enough to provide the necessary education. A responsible father must equip his children for life. This God has done, by leading the race from its lowest stages of mental and moral development to the present state of intellectual leadership.

God cares enough to discipline us. Does this thought fail to enthuse you? Then remember that a race without discipline is a race gone wild. What you are depends much upon human discipline. This is God's method also. He disciplines because He loves.

Does God care?. It would be better if we asked, "Do we care as much about our protection, development, provision and discipline as He does?"

WE'LL UNDERSTAND

We often wonder why disease
    Should stalk the earth,
Or famine, pestilence and want
    Be given birth;
But this we know, for us extends
    God's guiding hand,
And at His will, in His good time,
    We'll understand.

We may not see the need of grief
    Or constant strife;
Or sense the value of defeat
    That mars each life;
But may we rest assured that God
    Has all things planned,
And at the time He deems as best,
    We'll understand.

We shrink from pain, as well we may,
    'Tis hard to bear;
And falter when our lives are crushed
    By worldly care;
But trust in God, for He will give
    Us strength to stand;
And some day, when all things are bared,
    We'll understand.

We tremble at the thought of death,
    For us 'tis dark;
And fear the day, when at His will
    We must embark:
But then before us will arise
    A fairer Land,
And what, through life, we could not see,
    We'll understand.

God plans life well. He does not fail
    To note man's sin;
What brings us pain is born on earth,
    Not sent by Him;
Then trust, and know that He in love
    Doth still command,
And now—yes even now, through faith,
    We'll understand.

CHRISTIANS ARE DIFFERENT

We might not understand why some things happen but this we do know, that when the crisis comes, Christians are different. That was impressed upon my mind during the devastating flood, hurricane and tidal wave that visited New England, September 21, 1938. At that time I was Pastor of the churches at Baltic and Versailles, Connecticut. The destruction can be imagined by explaining that a river ran through the towns, and we were in the direct path of the hurricane. May I state briefly how religion aided in that crisis.

I saw calm in the face of turmoil. At 3 o'clock in the morning the alarm sounded. The river had overflowed and the flood waters were sweeping through the homes, yet there was an unusual calm in view of the grave situation.

I saw sacrifice in the presence of destitution. That afternoon the bridge separating the parsonage from the rest of the village was washed away. A little later the height of the flood and the force of the hurricane met and continued together, unabated for over two hours. These were the hours when sacrifice and the forgetting of self likewise reached their height.

I saw faith in the midst of destruction. Three services were held that first Sunday. One out of doors for those isolated from the village. The other two in homes throughout the day in Versailles and Baltic. To reach these homes I was forced to travel seventeen miles through tree-filled back roads, yet when the destination was reached, was only a stones throw from the site of the first service. All three were services of thanksgiving. That night I could say with great fervor, "Christians are different."

NOT DEATH, BUT LIFE

What beauty marks the over arching sky,
When from our view the sun sinks in the West;
We pause to watch the colors 'ere they fade,
And then with hearts aglow return to rest.

But yet we knew that when the sinking sun
Departed from our sight at close of day,
It did not die, but in another clime,
Still showered light and warmth upon its way.

What brush can paint the colors of the leaves,
When summer lengthens into early Fall;
We marvel at each leaf, its shape and hue,
And thank the One whose beauty touches all.

Yet when the leaves fall swiftly to the ground
As forests bow before the winter's storm,
We do not hail death as the conqueror,
For in the Spring we know new leaves will form.

And when our loved ones close their eyes in sleep,
We call it death, and falsely think that He
Who giveth nature life, would give but death
To those He loves the most, and yearns to see.

If God would part the veil that we might look
Beyond our little world of sin and strife,
We'd marvel at the change His hands had wrought,
For we would not see death, but only life.

THE LIFE THAT LIVES

This, and the next six poems, were written for funeral services. They are included with the hope that they will not only be helpful to ministers, but those for whom they were intended, all who mourn. Perhaps what I have in mind can be best presented by way of a few questions.

What is our relationship to the Divine? The entire Bible stresses the fact that we are His children, and the New Testament leaves the thought that we are His special treasure. During His ministry Jesus said, "Ye are my friends, if ye do whatsoever I command you." If we bear even these few words in mind, it will enable us to see clearly that we were not meant for death.

Would God look upon us as His children and special treasure, the Master consider us as His closest friends, yet at the end of life's little day cast us into an everlasting night? Even the most unworthy of the world would not do that to their children and possibly not to their dearest friends. And surely they would not seek to destroy their special treasure. Can we look at God and His Son and say that they would be guilty of that which is so repulsive to us? Let us rest assured, that because of our mutual relationship, the most elaborate plans ever devised, have been prepared for our future.

Do you suppose that God would have given His Son, and His Son His life for our salvation, if there was no place for us to go after being saved? If such sacrifice was made to redeem us, it was surely not for this short span of life alone. Only the most inhuman would save a person from one death, then cast him into the jaws of another. If death ended all, salvation might make the present tolerable, but would not be worth the price paid.

DEATH AS A FRIEND

Death comes on the wings of the morning,
    And gathers before the noon,
From out of the gardens before it,
    The fairest and sweetest bloom.
It may be that garden is ours,
    That bloom is the child of our love,
But fear not, it will be transplanted,
    In God's greater garden above.

Death comes in the heat of the noontime,
    When life is reaching its height,
And forcing the shadows before it,
    Illumines its presence with light.
For death does not come with its cowl,
    Or scythe or its skeleton hand;
It is life at its richest and fullest,
    The crowning arch in God's plan.

Death comes when the shades of the evening
    Encircle the ageing brow,
And kissing the cheeks worn and weary,
    It quietly whispers, "Now!"
And dropping the cares of a lifetime,
    And laying the earthly aside,
Our loved ones are clothed for that City,
    Where they will forever abide.

It may be the morn or the evening,
    Or noon when death will descend,
But behind the shadow that chills us,
    Is hidden the face of a friend.
For death is one of God's angels,
    Commissioned to gather when sent,
The beautiful souls of life's garden,
    Whose days upon earth have been spent.

Then fear not this friend when he cometh
    To earth 'midst its turmoil and strife,
For he does not ride on destruction,
    Or sever our loved ones from life.
But silently parting the curtains,
    Disclosing eternity's morn,
He bears them where death has been conquered,
    And they in Christ's likeness are born.

LIFE IN DISGUISE

In the last meditation some questions were raised for our consideration. Although known to all, in a day that gives birth to semi-skepticism, they need to be stressed often. Most moderns would not admit even a little skepticism, but have we not tolerated many of the prevailing doubts and allowed the confused thinking of the hour to so unsettle us, that we are not sure on many vital matters? For this reason I would like to ask a few more questions.

If God is love and Jesus His greatest expression of it, could death be strong enough to tear us away from that love? That is the confession we make when we question everlasting life. We are confessing that God is weaker than this one step in the process of life that He has planned. We are holding death as the master and the Creator as the slave. We furthermore stress, that the love of the Divine is of no avail. God's love from the beginning has amounted to little. The love of the Master is not strong enough to draw His disciples to His side in the future. The darkness of death has triumphed over the love of the Eternal. This we know cannot be true.

If the assurance of life everlasting given us by Jesus is true, then death is a friend. It may be the last enemy we shall conquer as earth views it, but anything that bears us to the bosom of Jesus is a friend.

We must live this life and live it well. We cannot assume an unhealthy attitude or false longing for the future to begin. Yet we must not hug fears to our heart concerning that which will inevitably come to all. May our faith rest on the eternal truth that death is the process used by God to lead us into life.

THE HEART OF DEATH

The heart of death is love,
And not some cruel stroke of fate,
That comes to crush the weak and strong,
On blackened wings of waste and hate.

The hand of death brings peace.
It touches us, and silently,
A gentle benediction gives,
That lasts throughout eternity.

What we call death is life.
Eternal life that knows no end;
And some day we will understand,
How perfectly the two doth blend.

The hope of death is Christ;
And in this hour of inward pain,
His promises assure us that
The faithful will unite again.

THE HEART THAT NEVER STOPS

Before his untimely death, Maltbie D. Babcock wrote,

> "Why be afraid of death as though your life were breath?
> Death but anoints your eyes with clay. O glad surprise!"

Why are we afraid of death? Is it because we fear the pain that very often accompanies it? This pain is real. To wish for it would indicate an unbalanced mind. Yet the greatest pain to be humanly endured, will pass into insignificance in the light of the other side. The fear of dying often surpasses the thrill of living with the Master.

Is it because we do not want to be separated from this life? We like this life. We rejoice in life itself. Because of its brevity we desire to cling to all there is of it. The life seen, looms larger on our horizon, than that which is unseen.

Is it because it places us in strange surroundings? We like the familiar. How we miss those enjoyments that have held for us a special attraction. The idea of a new world gives us a heartache long before the day of our transfer.

Is it due to fear that we will be removed from loved ones and friends? This, perhaps, is the most unwelcomed thought of all. But have we not heard from His lips of the relationship of loved ones and friends who dwell with Him?

Is it because of the impending judgement? Sin is in the world and from many directions it has touched our lives, and we wonder how we stand before Christ.

Whatever the reason, let us share this conviction together, that the heart of death is love, and love does not create, but banishes fear.

DEATH GIVES

Another loved one called of God
Has answered, and for us who stay,
Would bid us not to weep, for lo,
Death gives—it does not take away.

Death gives us rest. Rest undisturbed,
And free from sorrow, sin and pain,
That marred life's pathway while on earth;
A quiet rest that will remain.

Death gives us life. I know we weep,
And feel that life has been the price
Our loved ones pay when they depart;
But is it death to be with Christ?

Death gives—it does not take from us
This loved one we in sorrow mourn;
The eyes that now are closed in sleep,
Will wake to view Eternal Morn.

Death gives. It is not death to die;
Life's birth is always from above;
The God who gave has but recalled
Unto Himself, this one we love.

WHAT IS THERE LEFT TO DISCOVER?

What we call death is birth. We are not afraid of birth. How our hearts rejoice when a babe comes to grace our home? What love we shower upon him! Birth is ushered in by an outburst of joy and happiness. A child has been born into this life.

Death is birth into a fuller, richer life. When we were born into this world we received much. Birth into the next life will give us much more.

On our arrival here we received a world, a home, and loved ones. In other words, God had not only made all the necessary, but the most extensive preparation. We were not thrown into a cold barren world and left to struggle for our own existence. Waiting, were parents to receive, care for, and surround us with their love. Do you think for one moment, that God who so wonderfully planned this, has planned nothing for our birth into His greatest world? Ah, friends, rest assured that a greater reception will await us in that day than any reception that earth extended our way. If God can make the step into life so beautiful, will He not make the step into His presence even more attractive? Death is birth, and the pains accompanying it are birth pangs.

Of this we can be sure—death does not take anything from the Christian. Rather does it give far more than we are called upon to leave behind, when we at last close our eyes in this world that we might open them in the next. This marks the beginning of our greatest discovery.

THY WILL BE DONE

*Oh, you who mourn this solemn hour
    With aching heart,
Think you the hand of death can tear
    Loved ones apart?
This angel, death, meets every soul
    Escaping none,
But God plans well. Then let us say,
    "Thy will be done."*

*Death does not come with bony hand
    Or haunting face,
To smite, then hold your loved ones in
    Its cold embrace.
While it may cast its shadow o'er
    The brightest sun,
Look unto God with faith, and say,
    "Thy will be done."*

*Though slowly pass the painful hours,
    Without relief;
Fear not, for God is by your side;
    He shares your grief.
Remember that Eternal Life
    Has but begun,
And we must die to live. So sing,
    "Thy will be done."*

*Leave all to God, for He alone
    Doth understand;
He will not let you suffer more
    Than you can stand.
So trust His love and be assured
    Death has not won,
But God, who giveth Life. Then pray,
    "Thy will be done."*

FAITH FOR DESPERATE DAYS

Time is one of the most trying elements in sorrow. The weeks and months when our loved ones lie dangerously ill are hard to bear. Yet how short it seems, after health is regained, and they are returned once again to our bosoms! Even when we live through those painful hours feverishly tossing upon a hospital bed, what then seemed unbearable, looms as a dream when all is over. But how different the pain of sorrow! It continues through the days, weeks and years. Although conscious that our loved ones are safe in His keeping, the pain continues unabated. Time heals, but time is slow and we grow fearful lest we succumb.

Memory is another trying element. The noise of little feet that once sounded throughout the house never stills. The bright sparkling eyes, cheery, often impish smile, and continuous childish chatter, remain in the memory. Whenever a dear one has been called upon to change dwelling places, the remembrance of him remains fresh throughout the changing years. Every toy, every piece of clothing, every recurring incident, faces us daily and continues to open the wound that refuses to heal.

What shall we say for such an hour? Simply to plead for dumb resignation is futile. No one else can bear the pain that is ours. Even Jesus wept. These trying, desperate days call for faith. Our loved ones cannot be returned. We must rest in the fact that they are safe at last. No longer do we need to worry—for them. They are in God's care. Our will would have been different. Yet, through our sorrow, let us remember that we are being developed for a citizenship prepared only for those who are worthy.

SLEEP ON, BELOVED ONE

Sleep on, beloved one, sleep on,
We ask not that you be returned;
Though sad our hearts and drear our home,
Your peaceful sleep is justly earned.

Sleep on, beloved one, with Christ,
Securely guarded from all harm;
No more shall worldly baricades
Remove from you His shielding arm.

Sleep on, beloved one, in peace,
Far from the noise that marred life's day;
Sleep on! Rest well! This is God's will;
His angels now attend your way.

Sleep on, beloved one, we know
That it means life, not death to die;
Asleep in Jesus, yet alive
To all that Heaven doth supply.

Sleep on, beloved one, for now
You rest where all God's saints must dwell.
And so until we meet again,
We say "goodbye," but not "farewell."

AS HEAVEN VIEWS IT

Earth looks upon an incompleted scene. Heaven sees the completed picture. Ours is a half view. The full view is seen only from the other side. To stop at this is to miss the most important part of the Divine plan.

Heaven looks upon a life at rest. Although the poem might suggest the thought, rest doesn't mean idleness. How restful a book is to one who has labored through the day! Or some form of outdoor activity for the person working in office or shop! To rest is to do that which brings relaxation and enjoyment. Heaven is not a haven for the lazy. We shall "rest from our labors" to be sure, but this implies painful work. Heaven will be full of activity, but that which is painful is unknown.

Heaven bestows calm. The destructiveness of the hurricane is felt by all in its path. But after it is over, a quiet calm often settles upon the scene that was so turbulent. The calm is even more noticeable and effective than any that preceded, as though seeking to remind the world that God has not deserted. Death might strike with hurricane force, but for those in its path a quiet calm is certain to follow. Not the calm of a motionless death, but of life at its fullest, as Heaven views it. The peace that passeth understanding is always found in the presence of God.

Heaven provides hope with wings. Earth looks upon death as hope defeated. Plans for the future have been destroyed. "Why didn't God spare our loved one a few more years?" is the heart-rending cry. Heaven views the same experience, not as hope defeated, but fulfilled. Where Jesus is, hope is always to be found

HEAVEN

Earth with its beauty may ever attract us;
Earth with its sorrows gives birth to despair;
Yet we will learn how unchanging is Heaven,
When we shall claim our inheritance there:
Living consistently,
Free from all care.

Sweet our reception by earth, yet far sweeter,
Will be our welcome on that Golden Shore;
City of promise, where loved ones await us,
As we debark when life's journey is o'er:
Living triumphantly,
Peace evermore.

Drear is earth's valley and dark is its shadow,
Unlike the Land that destroyeth all fears;
City of comfort, where death never enters,
Sorrow is barred, and where falleth no tears:
Living constructively,
Down through the years.

Hail to that City our Father prepareth,
Dear to our soul though concealed from our sight;
City of refuge, our home through the ages,
Dwelling with Jesus who giveth it light:
Living eternally,
Knowing no night.

GOING HOME

I am very fond of any poem or song that expresses the thought of going home. I love to go home. After being away for a day the thought of returning is most refreshing.

Jesus said, "In my Father's house are many dwelling places—many homes. I go to prepare one for you." Heaven to me means home. I do not shrink from the thought, but rejoice in the fact that the place I love here—home—will not be denied, when for the last time I will lock the doors of my earthly house and move to one not made by human hands.

What makes home attractive? First, because it is the center of love. Love produces harmony, happiness, peace. We enjoy being where these reside. How much greater that love will be in the dwelling place prepared by our Master.

Home is a refuge, a sanctuary, a haven. It is a shelter from the world. There disappointments are forgotten. Fears fade. Happiness reigns.

Home becomes our personal workshop where we do that which we most desire to do. We do God an injustice when we sing of Heaven as a paradise for anemic, idle people. It will still be our workshop.

Home is the abode of loved ones. I cannot conceive of a hermit's house being a home. If love makes a home there must be loved ones to produce it. How inviting this makes Heaven.

Going home! How we rejoice in this thought at the close of day!

Coming home! That is the picture from the doorway of the dwelling place that awaits us.

Going home! That is all! Not dust! Not ashes! Not empty space, but home!

BE CALM, MY SOUL

Be calm, my soul, though faced with endless sorrow,
Wrought by unrighteous men whose souls have flown;
For God will have His turn with them tomorrow,
When they must face Him, naked and alone.

Be calm, my soul, amidst the worlds confusion,
Produced by man—all else obeys His will;
Fear not the mass who welcome sin's intrusion,
They too shall pass, then oh, my soul, be still.

Be calm, my soul, life's hour glass unfailing,
Reveals the coming doom of armored might;
His Kingdom only waits the great unveiling,
The present darkness but obscures its light.

Be calm, my soul, but rise with faith, persistent,
To break the chains of doubt, distrust and greed;
Be calm, but yet inspire a zeal consistent,
To work with Him until mankind is freed.

WATCH YOUR PULSE

We are all acquainted with the routine check-up, made at regular intervals, in our hospitals. It consists of taking the temperature and counting the pulse. These are nature's warnings. When the pulse becomes rapid there is danger ahead. However, it is not our hospitals alone that realize the need of this check-up. Life speaks daily, saying, "Watch your pulse!"

Joanne has a large shopping bag full of toys, consisting of those worn and soiled. Several times each week, this busy little three year old, takes the bag from its place and turns the contents out on the living room floor. She has been taught to pick them up and put them back when finished. One day, judging from her conversation and the uninterrupted dropping of toys to the floor, I knew she was having trouble. Leaving my study, I went down to find out what was wrong. There was her bag in the middle of the floor piled high with toys, yet there were many others for which she could find no room. Upon inquiring, I found that she had gathered up other toys that did not belong in the bag, and was making every effort to secure a place for them.

What a parable of life! We rush from one place to another gathering and filling our lives with this world's goods—mostly worn and soiled toys. And even after we have packed within everything we can hold, we still make a frenzied attempt to add the many other things still left. We need to be restored within, if our souls are to find the calm this turbulent hour demands. How true the words of the Psalmist, "The Lord is my shepherd I shall not want. He maketh me to lie down in green pastures. He restoreth my soul."

OUR THANKS

For blessings through another year;
For faith that masters human fear,
And peace from knowing Thou art near,
We give Thee thanks.

For courage in depressing days;
For guidance over wind-swept ways,
And trust that fills our hearts with praise;
We offer thanks.

For comfort that religion brings;
For hope, though tried, undaunted sings,
And strength to conquer baser things,
Accept our thanks.

For homes and loved ones held secure;
For friends and friendships that endure;
For Christ whose promises are sure,
We give Thee thanks.

Oh, God, whose plan of life we see
Unfold before us constantly,
This day we offer unto Thee
Our humble thanks.

EYES THAT SEE

Would it seem strange to give on this Thanksgiving Day an illustration from an Easter Sunday many years ago? Perhaps, but that is what I am about to do.

While a student at Boston University, I was for one year Assistant Pastor at St. John's Methodist Church in Watertown. I owe much to that year, especially to the Pastor, Dr. Francis Dee Taylor, whom I have always admired and loved. Among other duties, I was the teacher of a large boy's class. The class was composed of boys from our church homes and a group from Perkins Institution for the Blind.

That Easter Sunday the lesson concerned the Resurrection. It began with the resurrection in nature and led into the resurrection of Jesus and the assurance of life everlasting. However, as I finished the first section one of the blind boys, full of enthusiasm remarked, that the day before a group had gone on a hike through the woods with one of their teachers. His enthusiasm grew as he confessed, "Do you know, the trees and flowers were so beautiful that I did not want to leave." It was with difficulty that I finished the lesson, for my home was on the edge of that very woods, and I had walked the same paths every day. I had actually seen the trees and flowers that he described, yet did not possess his enthusiasm.

That was my greatest thanksgiving lesson, for I realized that if it was God's will that a blind boy should be so enthusiastic about something he had never seen, how much greater my enthusiam and thankfulness should be for the handiwork of God that greeted me every day.

149

THANKSGIVING THOUGHTS

I wonder how the Master feels
  While hearing each Thanksgiving Day,
Our prayer of thanks for peace and wealth
  Kind Providence has sent our way.

And as we plead for those whom fate
  Has placed where war and famine stalk,
Does He behold a broken heart?
  The absence of pretentious talk?

I wonder what the Master thinks
  Of our unwillingness to share
The struggles of subjected souls
  We wept for in our fervent prayer.

Perhaps if we could quietly
  Slip by His side where we could hear,
We'd find our prayer remained on earth
  And did not reach the Master's ear.

GOD SAVE AMERICA!

While on my vacation last year I followed for some distance one of the many automobiles that carried a large emblem, on which was an American flag and the words, "God Bless America.' I had no objections to the owner's display of his imagined or genuine patriotism. However, directly above this sign was another. It was even larger, more descernable and almost overlapped the former. The sign gave the name of an important Massachusetts dog racing track in large letters, and information concerning it, with dates of the races. This was the cause of my objections. He evidently had an interest in the park and was using this means of advertising it for his own personal gains. He was trying to stimulate public interest in gambling, thus making an appeal to the lowest instincts of man. He represented one of the thousands who yearly work for the undermining of American manhood and womanhood. He was one of an organized group leading to the destruction of the ideals of American life. As the two signs faced me I realized that the sign on his car should have read, "God Save America!"

This also attracted my attention. The sign on top was the one concerning the race track. His patriotic motto was given second place. Could it be possible that his racing interest came before his patriotism? That his country was worth blessing, providing it did not interfere with his lust for unholy wealth?

On this Thanksgiving Day, may we pray that God will save America from the forces that would destroy it.

A THANKSGIVING PRAYER

We thank Thee, Lord, for daily bread
    For work and peaceful rest;
For all the comforts, small and great
    With which our lives are blest.

We thank Thee for true brotherhood
    That fosters lasting peace,
And gives itself unsparingly
    'Till wars forever cease.

We thank Thee for each happy home
    Where harmony prevails,
That holds secure when baser hands
    Its sanctity assails.

We thank Thee for Thy templed halls
    Wherein we kneel to pray,
And learn with gladness to accept
    The challenge of each day.

We thank Thee too for Christian faith
    That guides our erring feet
To paths that wind their way at last
    Where life is made complete.

We thank Thee for the happy hours
    That follow through the years,
But may we not forget the balm
    Contained in sorrow's tears.

We thank Thee, Lord, for life itself,
    And may we gladly give
Ourselves in service to mankind,
    That we may truly live.

LET US GIVE THANKS

Let us give thanks for God. Without Him Thanksgiving would be impossible. Russia can never have a genuine Thanksgiving Day. A nation without God has no one higher than godless, sinful humans to thank, and who has ever received blessings from them?

Let us give thanks for everything God has showered upon our way. We cannot remember them all, but to forget even the least is ungrateful. God has been exceedingly good to the most undeserving. That goodness should not go unnoticed.

Let us give thanks for the strength, courage, hope and confidence that we received through pain, suffering and sorrow. This is the highest form of thanksgiving. A child appreciates the showers of blessings, even though he cannot understand the good contained in painful experiences. To be thankful for the lasting blessings that come through adverse conditions, distinguishes the genuine from the childish Christian.

Let us give thanks for everything we escaped this past year. If it has been a year of health, we have much for which to be thankful. If violence or destruction did not sweep down upon us, let us rejoice and give thanks. As many blessings come wrapped in the package labeled "What didn't happen," as in the one revealing what did take place.

Let us give thanks for Christ and Christianity. Once we were slaves. Now we are free. With blood upon our hands and sinful pursuits upon our mind, we went forth to meet both life and death. All this has now changed. Christ and Christianity has made the difference.

Let us give thanks!

OUR DREAMS

*Though our dreams excell all others
  In the novel and the new,
It will take a lot of hustle,
  If we make our dreams come true.*

*Though we start from early manhood,
  And we dream our whole life through,
It will mean less time for pleasure,
  If we make our dreams come true.*

*Dreams come dressed in silver linings,
  But they're dressed in shadows too,
And 'twill take a lot of heartaches,
  Ere we make our dreams come true.*

*I suppose all men are dreamers,
  But success comes to the few,
Who arise and work with fervor,
  'Till they make their dreams come true.*

DREAMERS, PLUS

Not all dreamers are to be exalted. There are some who dream their life away, leaving no contribution, either to their own lives or the world. Some never keep close to earth. They envelop themselves in haze. They become lost in clouds of their own making. Yet, men of vision are not to be condemned, because a few have failed to keep their feet upon earth. The great demand of the hour is for dreamers, plus. He who cannot dream, cannot create. When we lose our imagination we face stagnation. However, to be of value, dreams must be able to loom as large in the world as in the mind.

Dreamers are builders. Perhaps the person with the dream has done no more than reveal it to the world. Other minds have seen the value, and other hands have done the building. The real creator, nevertheless, is the one in whose mind that plan was first born.

Dreamers supply the dynamite of life. The laborer will not admit this. To him dreamers are either lazy or crazy. Yet, when the world needs to be stirred, who does it? Surely not suave politicians or reckless warriors. We rely too much upon them. When the world needs to be shaken God choses men of vision, and men of vision are dreamers. How harmless a preacher appears to the world! But a preacher with vision continually deals with dynamite. Poets have always been considered feminine, or at best queer, yet think of the dynamite poets have used.

Dreamers are trail-blazers and foes of self-complacency. They are filled with a constructive discontent. But merely to dream is insufficient. We must be dreamers, plus.

THE CONCEITED MAN

When you find a man conceited,
　　Wonder not, but mark this well,
That his mind has ceased to function,
　　And his head's begun to swell.

When he yearns for praise and glory
　　And his mighty deeds rehearse,
It's a sign his head is swelling,
　　But his mind's slipped in reverse.

When he boasts of his religion.
　　Based on platitudes and show,
It's because his head's expanded,
　　But his mind has ceased to grow.

When he thinks himself dictator,
　　Certain he'll not meet defeat,
Don't forget his head is swollen,
　　And his mind is in retreat.

When the mind has ceased its growing
　　We no longer can compel
Admiration for achievements,
　　So our head begins to swell.

THE WORLD'S PICTURE OF YOU

The world is the most persistent and successful photographer. It not only takes our picture, but publishes it before mankind. We might claim much for ourselves in the pictures we produce, but they are posed pictures. The world takes us as we are and our well worded claims and specially made pictures, fade into insignificance. Conceit ranks high among the many blemishes revealed in the world's picture, although it is never seen in the photograph we censor before we place on display.

Conceit is not the only indication that the mind is in retreat. Conceit in itself, apart from its relation to the mind, is not a pretty thing. It is a reminder that we have not grown. We are still childish.

Conceit is also an indication that we are not Christian. Christianity stands firmly against it. Jesus taught the opposite. So likewise did Paul and the other New Testament writers. Of all places where conceit should not be found is in the ministry, yet it is there, often in abundance. When we, as ministers of the Gospel, have to stretch our stories or forever dwell on our few better than average talents or achievements, it is a sign that we are no longer effective. We have either slipped or never did amount to anything from the beginning.

Conceit very often makes cry-babies out of individuals who have the appearance of men. Conceit always leads to jealousy. Jealousy produces the baby. God pity the minister who, jealous of another of his profession, allows this picture to stand forever before the world. That man has already defeated himself.

Conceit is the logical outgrowth of self-love, self-satisfaction, self-delusion. It is a poor attempt to bestow upon ourselves what others will not.

HAVE YOU COUNTED THE COST?

Oh, the work we leave unfinished,
*   And the precious hours lost,*
All because at the beginning,
*   We stopped not to count the cost.*

Have you ever seen a building
*   Half completed, left to rot,*
Showing that some thoughtless builder
*   Knew the cost, yet faced it not.*

Sad the souls who through the ages,
*   Forced by poverty and strife,*
Thought it best to make a living;
*   Thus they failed to make a life.*

Yes, abundant life is costly,
*   Yet so many start out well,*
But their tombs along the wayside,
*   Marked the spot they paused, then fell.*

Ah, the multitude of Christians
*   Bruised without and crushed within,*
All because they failed to ponder
*   The tremendous cost of sin.*

When the final call is issued,
*   Sad the going of the lost,*
Who have fallen short of Heaven,
*   Since they failed to count the cost.*

WHAT IS THE COST?

How much does it cost to follow Jesus? A hasty glance at some of His followers might suggest that the cost is slight. Even religious leaders have made their appeal on the basis of ease. "Live a good life. Unite with the church by answering a few questions and shaking hands with the minister." Thus the transformation from the worldling to a Christian has too long been a matter of mechanics rather than a changed life. The desertion of the church by youth has, in a large measure, been due to this Youth is attracted by the hard, not the easy. It demands that which costs.

This was not the appeal made by Jesus. He said, "If any man would walk where I walk, there are certain things he must do. To walk where He walked! Would not that be costly business today as it was in His day? To follow Jesus is not a matter of calling oneself a Christian—then walking where the world walks. It means doing what He would do. Going where He would go. Living as He would live. This would be costly!

How much does it cost not to follow the Master? We must not minimize the cost of following Jesus, yet how far greater the cost of not following Him? This we cannot afford to overlook, for the price is not for this short life only, but eternity. The wages of sin is counted in terms of unhappiness, despondency, suffering, death, in both this life and the next.

Have you carefully placed before you the cost of following Jesus in one column and the cost of not following Him in another? If not, will you do it? You will have no difficulty then in choosing which course to take.

"I HEARD" AND "THEY SAY"

Two popular idols that never die,
The great "I Heard" and the mighty "They Say,"
Chanced to meet one time on a quiet street,
And laughed and talked in a horrible way.

They greeted each other with well known signs,
And nodded their heads approvingly;
And who do you think they talked about?
Why, first about you and then about me.

The great "I Heard" had some stories to tell,
And he stretched and twisted them frightfully,
Until he blackened and tarnished the names
Of—yes, you guessed it! Of you and of me

And then the mighty "They Say" spoke up,
And not to be trumped by the great "I Heard,"
Unloaded MORE scandal, of course untrue,
Omiting not even a single word.

He told of the intimate things of life,
And emphasized each with apparent glee,
And the dirt flew high, and the mud grew thick,
As they talked about you, and also me.

At last they parted, these old time friends,
The great "I Heard" and the mighty "They Say,"
To gather more scandal and dig more dirt,
To use if they met on the following day.

Now who do you think these demons were
Who peddled scandal as though it were true?
Our mirrors will tell us. Let's look the next time
You talk about me and I talk about you.

THE WORLD'S GREATEST ASSASSINS

Have you looked through the rogues gallery in your local post office? I did some time ago. It was rather a complete collection. One folder had upon it the words, "Wanted for murder." Another, "Wanted for robbery." Still another, "Wanted for forgery," Then followed the usual description and pictures. What faces! Each face was a revelation of the sins committed.

Two of the most disreputable characters in this world are "I Heard" and "They Say." They are dangerous. If you can capture them, at least when they appear in your circle, hold them and never let them go. These are a few of the indictments against them.

1. They are wanted for murder. Their death blow comes at the point of one's character. They are more to be feared than those who would kill the body. A long distant telephone call is usual, but have you ever heard of a long distant murder? These friends do their murderous work at a distance, too far away to be detected.

2. They are wanted for robbery. Occasionally they mutilate but do not completely kill. They leave a little that is good, and then while unconscious, rob the victim of his choicest virtues.

3. They are wanted for forgery. Their right names are never used. Try and track them down! The result is futile.

Their faces? If you stand before them they will beam upon you. If you could see them as they are about to give the death blow, you would behold the hideous faces of treachery, deceit and cruelty. These are the world's greatest assassins.

A SELFISH MAN'S DREAM

A man who was selfish, conceited and small,
Dreamed sadly of having received his last call,
And thinking his boasting would cover his sin,
Called out to Saint Peter, "Sir, let me come in."

Saint Peter, politely, without much ado,
Looked out through the gate and said, "I don't know you
But lest I misjudge your true spiritual worth,
I'll call on the virtues who knew you on earth."

Benevolence entered at Saint Peter's call,
And eyeing the stranger, replied not at all;
But pressed for an answer, Benevolence sighed,
"He gave only when he had something to hide."

Then gratitude entered, and peering outside,
Looked long at the man who once strutted with pride,
And shaking his head he exclaimed with regret,
"I'm sorry, Saint Peter, but we've never met."

Saint Peter, astonished at what he had heard,
Called all of the virtues who came at his word,
And they, after looking the visitor o'er,
Replied, "We have never beheld him before."

Saint Peter looked solemnly out through the gate
And spoke to the stranger, in pity, not hate,
Informing him firmly ere letting him go,
The place he belonged was in Hades, below.

The man who was selfish, conceited and small,
Awoke from the dream that portrayed his last call;
And seeking a chance to begin life anew,
Prayed earnestly, knowing his dream to be true.

THE CURSE OF THE AGES

Forget the poem. It was not written as a serious effort. But don't forget the subject it concerns. Selfishness is the curse of the ages. It is seldom recognized by the person involved. What we call selfishness in another, is thrift or shrewd business sense in us. It is that which we condemn when we look out, and condone when we look within.

A greedy desire for gain is not the only form of selfishness. Whatever else is involved in a yearning for uncontrolled pleasure, this curse is involved also. That which enslaves, because we selfishly cling to it, we place before others that they too might become enslaved. Only unselfish men refuse to do that which might cause another to stumble.

Selfishness is involved in an unsatisfied lust for power. Dictators are selfish, ingrown individuals. The world has been cursed by a thirst for fame and power that recognizes no moral law, and destroys as it seeks to reach its goal.

To neglect one's own soul is selfishness. The person indifferent to his own spiritual condition, is a selfish, self-centered individual. Whatever he might say in his own behalf is meaningless, because the curse of the ages exposes him before the world.

To repudiate the church, to neglect the responsibility of financing the program of Christ, is an indication that selfishness abides in the heart. Nowhere is this felt more than in the Missionary realm.

As an antidote to selfishness listen to Jesus, "Seek ye first the Kingdom of God." If that is done, all the many needs of life will be provided, and the sins that condemn, will be unknown.

THE RICH YOUNG MAN

*I was the Rich Young Man who came to Christ
Long years ago when I was in my youth,
I sought the answer to Eternal Life,
And knew that He alone possessed the truth.*

*In earnestness I ran, lest He depart,
My spirit high, my haughty pride subdued,
And kneeling on the ground before His feet,
I seemed unconscious of the multitude.*

*I will not soon forget His look of love
As eagerly I said that from a lad
I had fulfilled the laws of God and man,
Yet ere I ceased His face seemed strangely sad.*

*"One thing thou lackest yet, my son," He said,
And then He paused and eyed me searchingly,
"Go sell thy goods and feed and clothe the poor,
Then take the cross and follow after Me."*

*My shoulders drooped, my eyes fell to the ground,
His words had pierced my heart as would a knife;
"Go sell!" Ah, no, I could not pay that price,
I loved my wealth—yes—even more than Life.*

*I stood, then turned and slowly walked away,
A sorrow none can know had gripped my heart,
The Master watched until I passed from view,
He knew that wealth and I would never part.*

*But now the weight of age has laid me low,
The hand of death is seeking mine to clasp,
And I am left alone with but my wealth,
When once Eternal Life was in my grasp.*

JUST A YOUTH

He was young. Youth is a crusader against wrong. This young man was anxious to fight certain sins, primarily those which he did not commit. But Jesus has a way of revealing our own personal sins as well as the sins of others, and this He told to the Rich Young Ruler. His sin was that of turning money to a god and worshipping it. When Jesus asked him to forsake that, he did not answer. His eagerness to eradicate sin had departed. Jesus had struck a bull's eye.

He was young. Youth demands that which is new and novel. He expected an unusual answer to his searching question. He was to be disappointed. Jesus was so old-fashioned in His approach! He said, "Give up!" Anyone could have told him that. That had been the message of the prophets. It was all so common-place. Yet how hard this common-place answer would have been if this young man dared to accept it!

He was young. The plans of youth are not full grown. He had his own ideas of life and Eternal Life. He had drawn his plans, but how small they were! The answer of Jesus was too big. "Sell what you have. Take up the cross and follow Me. Thou shalt have treasure in Heaven." This was too much for him. His conception of Eternal Life was worth some sacrifice, but not what Jesus demanded.

He was young. Youth so often leaves that which is of the greatest value and keeps that which is inferior. The Rich Young Ruler kept his wealth. That seemed to be of the greatest value to him. When he departed with it, he left behind him Christ and Eternal Life.

He was just a youth—the greatest reason why he should have accepted the program of Jesus!

TWO MEN

Two men went into the Temple one day
    To offer their prayer;
One was a Pharisee haughty and proud
    With satisfied air.

The other man quietly humbled himself.
    A publican he,
Who came not to boast of the good things he did,
    But God's face to see.

The Pharisee stood with a sneer on his lips
    And hate in his heart,
And carefully gathered his rich colored robes;
    To him 'twas an art.

The publican stooped lest his actions profane
    So sacred a place,
And the rays of the sun through windows of gold
    Illumined his face.

The Pharisee slowly lifted his eyes:
    His favorite pose,
And talked with himself instead of with God,
    In eloquent prose.

The publican, feeling the crush of the world,
    Without and within,
Unburdened his soul as he fervently prayed,
    "Forgive me my sin."

The Pharisee left with his usual sneer
    And satisfied nod,
Well pleased with himself for the fine things he said,
    But still minus God.

The publican, strengthened by way of his prayer,
    Prepared to depart,
And leaving the Temple he walked not alone,
    God dwelt in his heart.

And still as of old these two spirits invade
    God's Temple today,
And one enters only for boasting and show;
    The other to pray.

WATCH YOUR COMPANIONS

To live only with oneself is an indication that new companions are needed. Jesus suggests this in the picture He paints of the Pharisee in this parable. Even though his face is turned unto God, his eyes are focused on his own soul. Hear him as he tells God about the good things of his life, being careful to leave out the bad. He is in love with himself. It is a well established fact, that it is a sign of decay when we have to boast of our own goodness. This man, who looked so good without, had already decayed within.

His love for self made him forget his love for others. The more one thinks of self the less will he think of his fellowmen. When we place our ability or accomplishments above all else, the unworthy companion we live with is the only person we see. While we see the sins of another's life, we overlook the same kind and amount of sin in our own life.

His inability to see his own unrighteousness, caused him to look upon sinners with a sneer. The publican by his side was a sinner. He acknowledged it and pleaded for forgiveness, but the Pharisee only heaped contempt upon him. How callous he was, to be that near a sinner, yet feel no pain in his heart because of that sin! God forgive us when we are no longer concerned over the sin of our brother.

His vision was destroyed. He had looked within so long, he could not properly descern that which he saw without. When vision becomes destroyed, our feeling, love and helpfulness are destroyed with it.

How tragic it is when we feel we have all the religion needed! It is then we shut the door on God and our fellowmen, and live only with ourselves.

THE WIDOW'S MITE

She placed her gift on the altar,
  Then silently drew apart,
But more than two mites were laid there,
  For with it she laid her heart.

She gave two mites to Jehovah,
  Her wan face lifted above,
But she was the largest giver,
  For with it she gave her love.

And He who watched her in silence,
  Who knew the sacrifice made,
Praised her unselfish devotion,
  In words that never will fade.

WHAT MAKES ONE RICH?

The difference between this woman and ourselves is, that her mite represented all she had, while ours reveal that we have placed upon God's altar as little as we dare. It wasn't the amount of her gift, however, that brought commendation from the Master. Let us forget the two mites. We dwell so long on this point, that we become mite conscious, and give in proportion. That which has preserved her deed was the spirit behind the gift. Ordinarily, a poverty-stricken widow would give nothing. We would not expect her to. But her spirit prompted her to dedicate her money as well as herself to God.

Her spirit indicated she knew God. She was on familiar terms with Him. She had the utmost faith in His ability to protect and sustain her. All she needed was to lean on Him and He would provide the means and necessary strength to earn more. Her money reached the level of her highest thought.

Her spirit was an indication she knew others. She was acquainted with their needs. She understood their problems. Because of her meager store she could understand the hunger of those who did not share her faith in God. Her money followed her sympathies.

Her spirit indicated that she knew herself. She was weak. She had a secret desire to cling to that which she owned. She was conscious that her soul was ever in danger from this direction. Yet she knew that to succumb would make her small, selfish and useless. Her gift will always be a testimony, that she conquered the pagan passions that seek to master every life.

THE YOUTH I LIKE

I like the youth who faithfully
Attends his church each Sabbath day;
Who trusts in God instead of self
For guidance over life's rough way.

I like the youth who honestly
Prefers the high road to the low;
Who'd rather walk with God, alone,
Than seek the plaudits crowds bestow.

I like the youth who faces life
With body clean, and healthy mind;
Who loses self in Christian work
That he might better serve mankind.

I like the youth who fearlessly
Projects himself into the fight
For justice, peace and brotherhood;
Who stands unflinching for the right.

I like the youth who earnestly
Insists that he be straight and pure;
For when the years have taken toll,
He'll learn that these alone endure.

WHAT PRICE YOUTH!

Our young people do not always sense that life is exacting a definite price from them. There is an unnatural price that youth is called upon to pay, a price not of his own choosing. How much, for example, is youth worth as cannon fodder for war? What is the price tag the moving pictures place upon him? Or the liquor interest, whose desire is to develop a generation dedicated to intemperance? These are values, placed upon the unsuspecting, by well financed and organized groups.

That which I am interested in for this meditation, however, is the natural price expected from our young. Is it not true that youth is called upon to pay the price of his youth. The world has a right to expect much from those blessed with strength of body and mind. It is a responsibility that cannot be lightly cast aside.

Youth must pay the price of his convictions. He has convictions, real ones, dealing with the great issues of life. The spirit behind most worth while movements is the spirit of youth. Jesus paid a high price for His convictions, and He was a Youth.

Youth must pay a price for his courage. To follow Jesus requires courage, plus. His disciples realized this. It cost them a life of ridicule, suffering, and for the most part, a cruel death.

Youth must pay the price of his devotion. Devotion to the cause of righteousness requires sacrifice. We are living in a hard day, yet the hope of the world rests in the devotion of youth. The future depends upon the price youth is willing to pay today. It is a high price, but worth all it costs.

IF I WERE TWENTY-ONE

*If I were twenty-one I'd climb
The alpine heights of life, where I
Might catch a vision of the world,
And standing there midst earth and sky,
Would pray for strength and zeal to work
Down in the needy fields below,
And know that Christ would work through me,
If I but serve where He would go.*

*If I were twenty-one I'd stand
For that which Jesus would approve
If He were here to take my place;
Thus I would labor to remove
The evils that a worldly age
Have placed before its trusting youth;
I'd fight the lies of selfish men
Who gain their wealth distorting truth.*

*If I were twenty-one I'd live
My very best, and each new day
Would seek to be more like the One
Who is for youth, as age, the Way.
And I would strive to be a friend,
Not simply wear a friendly mask;
For this to me is love applied;
I view it as my Christian task.*

*If I were twenty-one I'd face
Approaching age with confidence,
Assured that righteousness in youth
Becomes the future's strong defence.
And thus if I were twenty-one
I'd dedicate myself to Him,
And live, that time might never see
My courage wane or vision dim.*

YOUTH TO MATCH THE AGE

There are two things we all enjoy doing. The first is, to give advice, and the second, tell what we would do if we were in the other man's place. Both are easy and very often cheap, yet that is what I am about to do in this meditation. I must confess, however, that at twenty-one I was not too successful in following the few thoughts suggested below.

If I were twenty-one, I would develop, prepare and equip myself for age. Age, at that time, seemed in the far-distant future to me. It doesn't now. Age has a way of creeping upon us, and the degree of health and happiness it brings, is largely determined by the preparation made in youth.

If I were twenty-one, I would challenge every questionable thought, suggestion or activity that faced me. This would not be easy, for the inexperience of youth, causes him time and time again to take the plunge, then ask the questions. I also recognize, that much I detest now, looked innocent enough at twenty-one.

If I were twenty-one, I would give my youth to Christ. I did it once. I would do it again. At eighteen I went to the altar and dedicated my life to the Christian ministry. I entered college at nineteen, through the guidance of my dear friend, Dr. Earl Marlatt, now Dean of Boston University, School of Theology. At twenty, I became Pastor of a little church nestled in the foothills of the White Mountains. Perhaps I have some right to present the advice given in this meditation.

YOUTH'S PRAYER

(Tune, "An Evening Prayer.")

To build a life that's clean, upright, secure,
God's temple that will through the years endure;
To walk courageously, steadfast and sure;
This is my prayer.

To teach a war-torn world the fruits of peace;
To plead that cruelty and hate must cease,
That earth might see goodwill and love increase;
This is my prayer.

To dedicate my life, my youth, my all
To Christ, and then in answer to His call,
Be faithful to each task—the large, the small,
This is my prayer.

YOUTH CAN PRAY!

This poem was written as a prayer hymn for young people's gatherings and institutes and has been used by such for several years. The intended purpose was to encourage the dedication of youth to higher service and lead to the realization that he possesses much that the church of today needs. A few of these needs are as follows:

The church needs the enthusiasm of youth. Enthusiasm is the power behind victory. Games have been won on the football field by the uncontrolled fervor of loyal rooters, and have been lost for the lack of it. Jesus was aware of this when He called youth and Zealots to be His disciples.

The church needs the daring of youth. The church has grown too timid. Daring is needed to surmount the difficulties the rest of us are unwilling to challenge.

The church needs the optimism of youth. When age says, "It can't be done!" youth replies, "Let me at it!" Just the over-confidence of youth? Yes, but this is the spirit behind forward progress in any realm.

The church needs the imagination of youth. Age moves carefully, on the basis of facts and past experiences. Youth is a natural pioneer, a dreamer. This is the foundation of discoveries and inventions.

The church needs the strength of youth. Youth craves a chance to exercise his strength. He wants the world to know what he can do.

It must ever be remembered, that the world will receive the benefit of these blessings, if the church neglects her opportunity. Youth does not have the only responsibility. The church has an even greater one. A church that neglects its youth is as guilty as a youth that neglects his church.

IF CHRISTMAS COMES

If Christmas comes, the peace the angels promised
Will be no longer but a prophet's dream;
When touched by Him, war's crimson, corpse-choked
    river,
Will be transformed into a healing stream.

If Christmas comes, goodwill will bind the nations
Into an understanding, perfect whole;
And never will distrust or racial hatred
Slink from their darkened haunts to wrest control.

If Christmas comes, it's Christ will find a welcome
In business, government and human heart;
And greed, injustice, fraud and self-indulgence,
The fruits of Christless living, will depart.

WILL WE BE READY?

How absurd! Christmas has been coming for over nineteen hundred years. It will come as usual this year. But will it? Christmas is not December 25, toward which we look with childish interest. That will come whether we live to see it or not. Christmas is bigger than any date or any period of celebration. It is a transforming experience. It will not come to us until Christ is born in our soul. This is likewise true of the world. It will be transformed this year only if Christmas comes to it. Whenever and wherever Christ is born there will follow that which followed His birth in a Bethlehem stable.

If Christmas comes, there will come to saddened hearts and a weary war-torn world, a joy equivalent to that which caused the shepherds to return from the manger "praising and glorifying God."

If Christmas comes this year, a spirit of love, big enough to embrace mankind, will come with it. "God so loved the world He gave—.' A little over thirty years later this story was once more repeated. Jesus, possessing the same love that was on the heart of God, gave His life for a similar purpose. The thought behind that love was, that it would include all men, at all times, everywhere.

If Christmas comes, there will follow a peace that will not only end war in our time, but make it impossible for war ever again to curse the world. "Glory to God—Peace on Earth." Present conditions are an indication that Christmas has not come to nations or multitudes of individuals.

If Christmas comes, salvation will replace the schemes of man, which from their very nature cannot work. Will we be ready to accept these gifts if Christmas should come?

A SHEPHERD SPEAKS

*I was a shepherd caring for my sheep
That starlit night when Jesus came to earth;
I little thought when darkness covered all
That I would witness such a holy birth.*

*We sat around as usual and talked,
And watched the stars, and dreamed of other days;
Not knowing that upon the sky we scanned
A scene none could forget would meet our gaze.*

*An eerie stillness settled o'er the hills,
A peaceful calm, unbroken through the night;
And as I now look back I can recall
That yonder David's town seemed strangely bright.*

*Then, suddenly there came a brilliant light
That turned the darkness into glowing day;
And we were sore afraid, and tried to hide,
Our lips were dumb: we knew not what to say.*

*'Twas then the shining sky seemed filled with life;
A tender voice fell softly on our ears,
"Fear not," it said, "To you no harm shall come,"
And in that moment hope replaced our fears.*

*The story from that point is known so well;
The guiding words, the hymn so strangely sweet;
Our visit to yon stable near the inn;
The Virgin's song; the Holy Child, asleep.*

*And then the journey back with hearts aglow;
How happy were our thoughts, how bright the way!
We praised Jehovah, singing psalms of joy,
For from night's depths emerged eternal day.*

IN WHICH DIRECTION ARE WE LOOKING?

In the second chapter of Luke we read, "There were in the same country, shepherds." To these humble, honest, reverent souls God spoke. Also in the same country were the indifferent, typified by the innkeeper and his guests. In the same country were the cruel, selfish and false, as seen in Herod and his followers. In the same country were the unbelievers, the multitude, who refused to accept Christ as God's Son, because of the place and manner in which He was born. But God did not reveal to them His divine plan. They did not hear His voice. However, in the very center of this mass of unbelievers were simple shepherds. They were sincere seekers after truth, anxiously awaiting the long promised Messiah. To them God poured out His message. They were facing the right direction, the direction of hope, salvation, God.

Today, too many of us are looking in the wrong direction for Divine instruction. Some are looking in the direction of scholarship, only to find that it is often divorced from religion, and the voice we hear is not pleasant to our ears. Others are looking in the direction of self-appointed saviours. Their windows are open towards Berlin, Rome, Moscow, Tokio, but instead of seeing a burst of light, there appears nothing but darkness. Still others look in the direction of custom and social sanction, and the sound that comes to them is the clank of the wine cup and the giddy laughter of the sons and daughters of shame. The noise and confusion entering these open windows will forever drown the voice of God.

But in the same country of our own day are devout souls. Though they will find it necessary to watch their flock this Christmas, their face will be turned toward God, and to them only will He speak.

NO ROOM

Room that first Christmas for sinner and saint,
Room for the stalwart and room for the faint,
Room for the prodigal, fleeing from home,
Room for the wanderer starting to roam,
But no room for Christ!

Room for forgotten ones, room for the great,
Room for the early and room for the late,
Room for the pilgrim to rest for the night,
Room for the wayward to cover his plight,
But no room for Christ!

Room for the master and room for the slave,
Room for the weakling and room for the brave,
Room for the burdened, so near to despair,
Room for the worldly—yes—room everywhere,
But no room for Christ!

Room for the millions today upon earth,
Whatever their faith, their station or birth,
Room for the war lords and criminals to live,
Room for mad pleasure—but yet do we give
More room to this Christ?

HAVE WE RECEIVED JESUS?

Christmas not only means giving. It also means receiving. We rejoice in this thought. Even though it is more blessed to give, we are nevertheless happy when we receive.

Would it be out of place to ask what we received this Christmas? The children would answer, "Candy and toys." The business man would point to his increase in business. All would gaze at the presents around the tree, and show them to the visitors as they called. Yet Christmas would not be elevated by these gifts, or our lives enlarged.

Receiving has a place in the Christian Christmas as important as that of giving. The true spirit of the day would be impossible apart from this. It is not the material gifts that we have in mind, but rather the One who is the life and light of this sacred season. Have we received Jesus? If not how unfortunate we are, even though we might be surrounded by material gifts!

Have we received Jesus in our thoughts? The innkeeper and his guests enjoyed themselves that night eating, drinking and joking. They had no room for Jesus because this was more alluring. The mind that has no place for the Master becomes an inn dedicated to the coarse and vulgar.

Have we received Him in our home? Life will become unbearable and happiness will depart from a home that has made no room for Christ.

Have we received Him in our heart? Heart trouble seems to be on the increase, but it is not confined to the physical area of life. Spiritual heart trouble is on the increase too, and as in the case of the former, it is most dangerous. Of this we can be sure, death is at the end of both.

WHY DID GOD SEND HIS SON?

Why did God send His Son?
To tell us how to decorate
Our windows, lawns and Christmas trees?
Or how the well-dressed Santa Claus
Should learn to entertain and please?

Why did God send His Son?
To teach us how to swap our gifts
And pick uncommon Christmas cards?
Or eat the season's choicest foods
And send the smartest "best regards?"

Why did God send His Son?
That men might use, through pious ads,
This sacred day to sell their wares?
Or plan gay parties, drunken brawls,
That earth-bound lives might drown their cares?

Was it for this God sent His Son?
For this He suffered such a loss?
If so, then may we soon forget
Both Bethlehem and Calvary's cross!

WE KNOW THE ANSWER, BUT — !

We live and act as though we have never heard. Business knows the answer, yet the biggest business opportunity of the year looms larger with many than God's greatest gift to the world.

Pleasure devotees know why God sent His Son, yet to them Christmas means a time for self-indulgence, drink and lust. Their interest centers around a good time rather than a good life. The song of the angels was one of joy. Theirs is one of gaiety—a gaiety that ends in riotous living.

The multitude knows. But the giving and receiving of gifts seems to eclipse all else, and when the day ends there is nothing left for Kingdom causes.

We know the answer, but sometimes we forget. This meditation is not intended to suggest that the material side of Christmas should be ignored by the Christian. Honest business men are needed at this time of the year. Without gifts, trees and lights Christmas would be drab and drear. The thought intended is, that we must not become so infatuated with the material, that Christ will be forced to accept our left-overs of love and possessions.

The world is looking in our direction to determine how much we, who know the answer, care. It is wondering whether we will put Christ first. It is listening for our words of appreciation and thanksgiving. It is looking to see what effect Christmas will have upon our lives. The way we react, will decide to a large measure, how it will eventually act.

We know the Christian answer to the question, "Why did God send His Son?" May we not be guilty of giving pagan answers through our actions.

BECAUSE CHRIST CAME

*Because Christ came
A faith has been engendered:
All nations bow in reverence at His name;
The hearts of men are everywhere rejoicing,
And all of life is changed—
Because Christ came.*

*Because Christ came
The day of peace draws nearer:
The day when war no more shall kill and maim;
We offer up a prayer of true thanksgiving,
Assured that day will come—
Because Christ came.*

*Because Christ came
Faith, hope and truth have conquered;
The dying brands of love fanned into flame;
And not by might, but gentleness, His Kingdom
Will come to stay on earth—
Because Christ came.*

WHAT HAVE WE GIVEN?

What have we given this Christmas? If we have given only elaborately prepared presents we have done nothing distinctive or new. Do not the publicans and sinners the same?

To whom have we given? Only to relatives and friends? Is not this what pagans do, and all men have done from the beginning of time?

To whom did God give when He gave His Son? His gift of a Saviour was not only to friends, but His enemies as well. His friends would rejoice. His enemies would retaliate with abuse. Yet this did not stop Him or cause Him to narrow the circle of those to whom Jesus was to minister. The greatest of all gifts was to the most undeserving as well as the most deserving. Does our giving match His?

We cannot give presents to everyone. We cannot even send them all cards. But we can give a greater gift—ourselves. Not to friends only, but in service to all men.

We can give love. It is easy to bestow love upon the lovely, but Christmas demands that we give it to the unlovely as well.

We can give hope and encouragement. It may not seem much to us, but it might mean life to others.

We can give forgiveness. Someone has wronged us. Someone has been unkind in word and act. We cannot stop them, perhaps, but we can forgive.

Thus at Christmas, as far as is humanly possible, we can match the love of God by bestowing love's greatest gifts upon friend and enemy alike.

THEN AND NOW

(A Christmas Meditation.)

When Christ was born, though passing years
 Saw hope depart,
A thoughtless world refused Him room
 Within its heart;
But war, injustice, cruelty,
 Each had their place,
And church and nation joined to fleece
 A bleeding race.

Since then the world has reached new heights
 In thought and deed,
Yet war, injustice, cruelty,
 Find room to breed;
And church and nation still combine
 When prophets rise;
With Christ rejected through intrigue
 And compromise.

BABE OR SAVIOUR, WHICH?

There are many who will not like this poem. "A pessimist," they will say. "One blind to the progress of Christianity. Doesn't he know that 'All's right with the world'?"

This I do know, that if we become so satisfied we can look out upon the world this Christmas and not see the injustice, cruelty, war, intrigue and downright sinfulness, then we will be blind indeed. Civilization has advanced. Whatever goodness there is, and there still is an abundance of it, is here because that first Christmas revealed Christ to the world. I am aware of all this, yet how dare we rest when unrighteousness is so rampant! Even if the underlying thought in the poem has been slightly exaggerated, is it not necessary, in a day when the world has dedicated itself to minimize evil?

Why is it, that after nineteen hundred years, the very sins He came to eradicate still flourish? May not this be the answer? At Christmas we piously worship the babe in the manger. We sing our anthems of joy—all concerning a baby. The next day we go forth to be the same narrow, sinful individuals as before. Why? Because the day before we knelt before a babe. A babe that could not speak, that could not remind us of our sins. One to whom we could pay tribute, yet do, as we please.

Have we forgotten that this babe grew into manhood? That His sweet cooing changed to words, that if followed, would result in the transformation of the world? Perhaps the reason pagan conditions flourish is because we have listened to His cooing, but not His words.

THE LEADERSHIP OF LOVE

If I allow the sordid things
  Of life to press
Me to their bosom without sign
  Of inward stress,
My actions tell, however suave
  My words might be,
That what I love has claimed not part,
  But most of me.

If I bestow on greed or gold
  Approving nods,
I then confess that I adore
  Earth's lifeless gods,
And worship them, no matter what
  I might disclaim,
Accepting God, not with my heart,
  But just in name.

But if I yield myself to Christ
  And with each day,
Give unto Him the love that earth
  Now takes away,
His will would then be my concern,
  For this I know,
That where I place my love, there too,
  My heart will go.

RESERVE RESISTANCE

During the first conversation I had with the doctors, at the Martha's Vineyard Hospital, they said, "For approximately the first two days Mrs. Wiseman will live on the resistance she had when she entered, but from the third day on she will live on her reserve resistance. This will go a long way in indicating her ultimate recovery."

"Reserve resistance!" These words registered in a different way at that time than they do now, because I was not sure how great her reserve resistance was. But today they speak another language. They speak not only to my body and mind, but my soul.

How much reserve resistance have I? When temptations come, will I weaken, or will my reserve resistance carry me through? When I face the hour of crisis and my mental resistance is lowered, what then? It is not difficult to apply this to every problem, situation or spiritual danger that faces my life daily.

The reserve resistance of the soul must be developed. There are vital vitamins for the spiritual life as well as the physical. If I overlook or neglect them I will not be prepared when the deluge descends.

The building up of one's reserve resistance is a, requirement. It is the least the Master expects of His followers. Even a casual glance at His words will indicate this. To fail in this respect, is not only to fail ourselves, but Him.

If I allow the sordid things of life to press me to their bosom, not only my fellowmen, but the Great Physician will know that my reserve resistance is minus.

A VOICE FOR GOD

No longer do I view my task
    As someone sent
To listen to the voice of God
    Then rest content;
But as I walk where wind-swept trees
    And flowers nod,
I know that I, like them, must be
    A voice for God.

God has a message for this age,
    A timely word,
But only souls attuned to Him
    Can make it heard;
Then let me be a voice for God,
    Let me convey
To faithful, yearning souls, His thought
    For this tense day.

The narrow vision earth beholds
    Must end in doubt,
For faith that burns on what is seen
    Soon flickers out;
So this I ask as through the years
    I daily plod,
That I might live and bless the world—
    A voice for God.

LET GOD SPEAK

To be a voice for God sounds easy. All one needs to do is open his mouth and speak. There are many who even dispense with the few easy lessons someone indicated were required. Consequently, individuals who claim to be God's mouthpiece can be found everywhere.

This is one of the world's greatest tragedies, for from this material "crackpots" are made, and at least one or more are to be found in every church and community. No greater injustice can be done God than to have one of these poor, self-deluded, misguided "Christians" claim to speak for the Almighty.

When a shallow or unbalanced person suddenly declares that he has received a special revelation or message from God, beware. There is trouble ahead, and his announcements are the storm warnings. But this is not confined to single individuals. There are sects abroad who defy the world to persecute them, so sure are they that God speaks only through them.

To be a voice for God requires, that behind the voice, is the most levelheaded, well-balanced person in the universe. Added to this must be genuine, not imagined consecration, ability, tact, courage, and above all, an intensive period of training. No one can speak effectively for God with a training that comes overnight.

Yet, in spite of what has been said, everyone can hold this office. Many of the most successful never had the advantage of higher education. This, however, must be clear. When one undertakes to speak for the Divine, he must be sure that he is not unloading upon society some pet theory or dark age dogma. God is sinned against, more effectively oftentimes, by those who claim to serve Him, than by His enemies.

THE MEANING OF YESTERDAY

Yesterday came with its sunlight and shadows,
Scattering happiness, fostering strife;
Now with its passing we search for the answer,
What did our yesterday mean to our life?

Yesterday came with its doubts and its failures,
Shaking foundations that long held secure;
But in the hush of the night, faith had taught us,
Only through Christ come the things that endure.

Yesterday came with its sorrows to open
Deeper and wider the wounds of our heart;
Bitter our anguish, yet clear was its message,
Life would be feeble had sorrow no part.

Yesterday came with its clouds and its sunshine,
Weaving together both laughter and tears;
Yet in the twilight we read what was written,
Yesterdays fit us to master the years.

THANK GOD FOR YESTERDAY!

Yesterday has a meaning. Although in the past, its shadow stretches ever before us. If we view the future with expectancy, it is because yesterday has provided us with a proper foundation. If there appears to be only hopelessness before us, perhaps it signifies that we allowed the days of the past to go unchallenged.

Do not our yesterdays teach us the value of time? They were the present day once. Now they are gone. When they were fresh, did not life appear as being of endless duration here? Most of life was before us. We sensed neither its value nor the value of time. But now as we view the years gone, and the relatively few left, we realize how precious time is.

Our yesterdays have taught us, that the big question of life is not, "What can I get for myself?" but rather, "How can I be of service to others?" We have found that happiness does not come through grasping, but unselfish giving.

Has not yesterday taught us, that we possess nothing unless we possess ourselves? We know that our greatest mistakes have resulted because we lost possession of ourselves. When we conquered ourselves we conquered our most persistent foe.

Yesterdays are a reminder, that to fail Christ, is to fail. He is the Way, the Truth and the Life. If we have not discovered this, we have failed.

But yesterday warns us to make the best of tomorrow. Whatever the past, tomorrow is as unsoiled as God Himself. Our Christian duty is to keep it such.

THE PASSING YEAR

*Another year has swiftly passed,
Its grandeur fades before our view
As through the open gates we walk,
From out the old into the new.*

*Another years has dimmed its light,
And drawn its shade forever more,
And never will the world again
Unlock that barred and guarded door.*

*Another year has waved good-bye,
And said farewell to humankind:
Yet all the lessons that it learned
It does not take, but leaves behind.*

*Another year has claimed its share
Of loved ones we have lost awhile,
But it has also showered love
In answer to each new babe s smile.*

*A brand new year is now before.
It's brilliant light reveals the dawn,
Reminding us, that though we rest
The wheels of time move ever on.*

WHAT SHOULD DIE WITH THE DYING YEAR?

The end of the year! There are many who will look back wistfully, sorry to see it go. They will remember the opportunities and happiness it brought. There are others who will be glad. Perhaps they feel the year has been unkind to them, or they have become sick at heart because of the turmoil, confusion, and bloodshed that have marred every day since its beginning.

Although we face tomorrow with confidence, let us not deceive ourselves into thinking that a new year will mean a new order of things. This year began with the same hilarious celebration that started other years. It was born amidst well wishes of the multitude, and prayers of a better day by the faithful. Yet suffering, war and famine have continued throughout. To think that a new year is of itself capable of changing conditions, is rank superstition. It is not a new year the world needs, but a new spirit. Without that there is no hope.

The end of the year! Let it go, but not empty handed! This we would ask it to do:

1. Take with it the suspicion, hate, bitterness and misunderstanding that dogged its pathway.

2. By all means carry war away and bury it forever. This is a most vicious and pagan curse, yet it usually rears it head in a supposedly Christian world.

3. Destroy everything unsocial, that works to the disadvantage of the least of our fellowmen, all that keeps us from God, and delays His Kingdom.

We look forward to a new spirit for humanity, a new heart for the world, a new life for man, and a new emphasis upon the Master and His plan of salvation.